Mozart's

THE MAGIC FLUTE

OPERA CLASSICS LIBRARY™

Edited by Burton D. Fisher
Principal lecturer, *Opera Journeys Lecture Series*

Opera Journeys Publishing™ / Coral Gables, Florida

OPERA CLASSICS LIBRARY ™

• Aida • The Barber of Seville • La Bohème • Carmen
• Cavalleria Rusticana • Così fan tutte • Don Giovanni
• Don Pasquale • The Elixir of Love • Elektra
• Eugene Onegin • Exploring Wagner's Ring • Falstaff
• Faust • The Flying Dutchman • Hansel and Gretel
• L'Italiana in Algeri • Julius Caesar • Lohengrin
• Lucia di Lammermoor • Macbeth • Madama Butterfly
• The Magic Flute • Manon • Manon Lescaut
• The Marriage of Figaro • A Masked Ball • The Mikado
• Otello • I Pagliacci • Porgy and Bess • The Rhinegold
• Rigoletto • Der Rosenkavalier • Salome • Samson and Delilah
• Siegfried • The Tales of Hoffmann • Tannhäuser
• Tosca • La Traviata • Il Trovatore • Turandot
• Twilight of the Gods • The Valkyrie

WEB SITE: www.operajourneys.com E MAIL: operaj@bellsouth.net

"It takes more culture to perceive the virtues of
The Magic Flute text than to point out its defects"

-Wolfgang von Goethe

Contents

a *Prelude*........
to OPERA CLASSICS LIBRARY's
THE MAGIC FLUTE

THE MAGIC FLUTE possesses many levels of interpretation: it is a fairy tale in which moral forces struggle against evil; it is a political and social allegory of late eighteenth century Austrian politics; it is an archetypal story of man's elevation to consciousness and awareness; and it is an exposition of the ideals of Freemasonry. Mozart's sublime music score emphasizes the opera's underlying intellectual elements; those noble sentiments of freedom, truth, and human brotherhood that pervaded the minds of men of intelligence and goodwill during the Enlightenment, that would reach their full fruition in the French Revolution of 1789.

OPERA CLASSICS LIBRARY explores the greatness and magic of *THE MAGIC FLUTE.* The *Commentary and Analysis* offers pertinent biographical information about Mozart's mind-set at the time of the opera's composition, the genesis of the opera, its premiere and performance history, and insightful story and character analysis.

The text also contains a *Brief Story Synopsis, Principal Characters in The Magic Flute,* and *Story Narrative with Music Highlight Examples,* the latter containing original music transcriptions that are interspersed appropriately within the story's dramatic exposition. In addition, the text includes a *Discography, Videography,* and a *Dictionary of Opera and Musical Terms.*

The *Libretto* has been newly translated by the Opera Journeys staff with specific emphasis on retaining a literal translation, but also with the objective to provide a faithful translation in modern and contemporary English; in this way, the substance of the drama becomes more intelligible. To enhance educational and study objectives, the *Libretto* also contains music highlight examples interspersed within the drama.

The opera art form is the sum of many artistic expressions: theatrical drama, music, scenery, poetry, dance, acting and gesture. In opera, it is the composer who is the dramatist, using the emotive power of his music to express intense, human conflicts. Words evoke thought, but music provokes feelings. As such, opera's sublime fusion of words, music, and all the theatrical arts, provides powerful theater, an impact on one's sensibilities that can reach into the very depths of the human soul.

Mozart's *THE MAGIC FLUTE* is a work possessing serene spirituality; it remains a masterpiece of the lyric theater, and a tribute to the art form as well as to its ingenious composer.

Burton D. Fisher
Editor
OPERA CLASSICS LIBRARY

THE MAGIC FLUTE

"Die Zauberflöte"

A *Singspiel* Opera in German in two acts

by

Wolfgang Amadeus Mozart

Libretto by:
Emanuel Schikaneder and Carl Ludwig Giesecke

Premiere:
Wiedener Theater, Vienna,
September 1791

Commentary and Analysis

*T*he Magic Flute is a supremely outstanding operatic work, whose underlying story provides various interpretative probabilities. Its basic story is essentially a fantastic fairy tale that is imbedded with mystery, sorcery and witchcraft. In that sense, its underlying conflict, the Queen of the Night against Sarastro in a battle for the custody and education of the Queen's daughter, Princess Pamina, can ultimately be viewed as a power struggle between the forces of good against the forces of evil.

The Magic Flute is also an allegory clothed in the ideals of Freemasonry: its story provides an idealistic portrayal of humanity's struggle for truth, wisdom, and nobility, and the adversity and self-sacrifice inherent in achieving those goals. But in the 18th century, Freemasonry was a secret brotherhood that was in conflict with the uncompromising Austrian Hapsburgs. As a political and social allegory, the story therefore represents a veiled assault on the autocratic rule of Empress Maria Theresa, who was known for her intense passion in suppressing Freemasonry: in that sense, Maria Theresa appears allegorically as the Queen of the Night; Prince Tamino as the Emperor Josef II, a defender of the secret order; and Pamina as the Austrian people who were caught in the conflicting political struggle. A final interpretive possibility is that *The Magic Flute* is synonymous with mythological tales in which classical archetypes, in conflict with mighty adversaries, are nurtured to maturity and elevated to consciousness.

That variety of interpretations and underlying meanings of *The Magic Flute* provide one reason for the opera's endurance for over two centuries. Nevertheless, viewing the whole as well as the sum of its parts, *The Magic Flute* is a truly magical blend of noble social and political ideas, mythology, mystery and magic, romance, and even comedy/ All of these elements are ingeniously underscored with Mozart's extraordinarily sublime music.

*I*n May 1791, Mozart's old friend from Salzburg, Emanuel Schikaneder (1748-1812), actor, singer, and somewhat jack-of-all theatrical trades, commissioned him to compose *The Magic Flute* for his suburban Viennese playhouse, the *Theater auf der Wieden* ("The Wiedener Theater"). Schikaneder was convinced that from a theatrical point of view, *The Magic Flute* story was powerfully attractive: likewise, there was but one composer qualified to endow it musically, and that was his friend Mozart. The new opera was to be a *singspiel*, the traditional German song-play with spoken dialogue. Although it did indeed follow those theatrical conventions, it evolved quite differently from the *singspiel, Die Entführung aus dem Serail* ("The Abduction from the Seraglio"), that Mozart had recently composed in 1782.

At the time, Mozart was in dire financial straits. Joseph II had died in March 1790, right after the premiere of *Così fan tutte,* and the new emperor, Leopold II, lacked the idealism, imaginative sympathy, and love of music of his predecessor. In effect, Mozart's loss of royal patronage had placed him in a desperate financial situation; in particular, his mounting debts, and Constanze's new baby. The 40 year-old Schikaneder was likewise in the midst of one of his many periods of financial embarrassment, and his profound belief in the viability of *The Magic Flute* offered him a possibility for financial recovery.

At the same time, Mozart was yearning to write an opera in German, something he had not done since *Die Entführung aus dem Serail.* Nevertheless, he desperately needed a librettist to inspire him. Lorenzo da Ponte, the venerable librettist for his recent successes, *The Marriage of Figaro, Don Giovanni,* and *Così fan tutte*, was no longer available: da Ponte, soul-mate of the illustrious Casanova, had been obliged to leave Austria because of his notorious and scandalous escapades with women.

But it was Schikaneder who became the spiritual force guiding *The Magic Flute* to fruition. Schikaneder's art and life seemed to be fused. He came from a childhood of immense poverty, became an itinerant fiddler, and then an entrepreneurial manager, eventually graduating to acting; he toured in his own company portraying the title roles in *King Lear, Macbeth*, and *Hamlet.* But his theatrical legacy remains controversial: he has variously been regarded as an errant rogue as well as a wayward genius. Nevertheless, at heart he was the consummate showman, a man who possessed good theatrical instincts and read his audience's pulse well: he always provided his audiences with what they wanted — musicals, rodeo — or any attraction that would result in paying customers even though the ultimate result might descend into vulgar entertainment.

Schikaneder was convinced that the fairy-tale, *The Magic Flute*, would not only have great appeal to his audiences, but that it would indeed become a financial success: it contained ancient mysteries and magical themes, all of which, were very much in the current vogue. *The Magic Flute's* plot was also an ideal theatrical vehicle: it was filled with a magnificent conflict of good versus diabolical forces, the ultimate triumph of love, and at the same time, it provided for burlesque characters in an exotic Oriental setting. Notwithstanding, the fairy tale aspects of the story provided Schikaneder with the opportunity to produce his trademark lavish theatrical spectacle, such as elaborate stage machinery, live animals, and ambitious lighting, effects which he cleverly interspersed with vaudeville-style comedy and songs.

In the end, Schikaneder's *The Magic Flute* became an inspiration for Mozart: it was a work that was saturated with a magnificent combination of allegorical symbols, subtle satire, love, romance, humor, and an opportunity for the display of theatrical wizardry.

T he plot of *The Magic Flute* evolved from a pseudo-oriental genie-type of tale, *Lulu,* or *The Magic Flute,* originating from a collection published by Wieland in 1789 under the title *Dschinnistan.*

Schikaneder, Mozart, and a flamboyant actor, Carl Ludwig Giesecke, the latter, the pseudonym for Johann Metzler, a versatile lawyer and sometime Professor of Mineralogy and Chemistry at the University of Dublin, were the collaborating librettists: coincidentally, all were members of the same Viennese Freemason lodge, although it is reputed that Schikaneder had been earlier expelled for his philandering.

Schikaneder's initial conception for his "magic" opera placed the simple fairy tale plot in an exotic Oriental setting. But as the story developed, modifications were made, and the venue was transplanted from the Orient to ancient Egypt. It had been theorized that the change of venue was made to avoid competing with another fairy tale opera that featured magical musical instruments in an Oriental setting: *The Magic Zither,* by Schikaneder's rival, Marinelli. However, contemporary musicologists have discarded that theory: it has been determined that authors in those days cared little about the originality or freshness of their fairy tale operas; they cared only about spectacle. Further, it has been determined that Mozart saw *The Magic Zither* and considered it a worthless play; thus, the sharing of a similar subject was inconsequential.

Now, the writers had transplanted their original story's locale to ancient Egypt. Freemasonry's roots evolved from ancient Egypt, and the librettists as well as the composer were Freemasons, who, by design, specifically intended their story to include much Masonic ritual and symbolism. The simple fairy tale that originally dealt with a power struggle between the forces of good and evil and the ultimate triumph of love, was ultimately transformed into a highly complex allegory glorifying the ideals of Freemasonry: inherently and implicitly, the story would become a satire and allegory that would address Freemasonry's contemporary political struggles for survival within Austria.

Many musicologists have hypothesized that many of the events in the opera derive logically from Masonic laws and rituals, all of which, Mozart and Schikaneder were very profoundly familiar with: in particular, the solemn choral scenes involving Sarastro and the Priests, and the impressive fire and water ordeals, all of which, are patterned after Masonic rituals and symbolism. In the end, a simple good vs. evil fairy tale story evolved into a mini-saga containing spiritual Masonic ideologies, that also incorporated political and allegorical satire, and even archetypal mythological significance.

The story contains many unique and dramatic character transformations: characters who are deemed evil during the first part of the story — Sarastro and the Priests — suddenly turn out to be virtuous and wise, and those who are initially deemed to be virtuous — the Queen of the Night and the Three Ladies — become the embodiment of wickedness and evil. Those character reversals provide the plot with intensely dramatic moments of conflict and tension: the Queen of the Night becomes a potent counter-force against Sarastro. Her wickedness and obsession for revenge compel her to command her daughter Pamina to commit murder , and when that fails, she invades Sarastro's stronghold with similar intensions.

In the opening scenes, the Queen of the Night and her Three Ladies are ostensibly noble and sympathetic characters: they are sincere, righteous, morally above reproach, benevolent, and compassionate. The Queen has an obviously legitimate grievance against Sarastro, the man who forcibly kidnapped her daughter, Pamina. The Queen's anguish and despair are expressed in powerful words, and in profoundly dramatic music; Mozart used his traditional technique of the coloratura style to express these excessive passions. The Queen tells Prince Tamino how her daughter trembled and cried for help while she was being kidnapped: "Noch seh ich ihr Zittern mit bangem Erschüttern, ihr ängstliches Beben, ihr schüchternes Streben" ("As a scoundrel abducted her, I still see her shiver, tremble and quiver, with no strength to resist.") And as the Queen reveals the story, she condemns Sarastro as a powerful sorcerer and the incarnation of all evil.

The Three Ladies initially uphold the standards of morality by punishing Papageno for lying about killing the serpent. But they pardon him, remove the padlock from his lips, and then deliver the first of many pious exhortations that makes the opera story a seemingly classic fairy-tale morality play: "If only all liars would get such a padlock on their mouths, we would have love and friendship instead of hate and slander." Similarly, those same Three Ladies furnish Tamino with a magic flute that possesses divine powers and will protect and safeguard him in danger. They tell him, "You can reverse human suffering and convert sadness to happiness, and assure that the loveless will always be loved."

The opening scenes of *The Magic Flute* are weighted with powerful expression of male chauvinism and antifeminism: the struggle seems to be concerned with worthy male virtues opposed to less worthy female virtues.

The Queen has already persuaded Tamino that Sarastro possesses monstrous evil; thus, filled with sympathy and compassion for the Queen, Tamino easily becomes her instrument for revenge. But Tamino will shortly face contradictions in his beliefs. After he arrives at the temples in Act I - Scene 3, the Elderly Priest listens patiently as Tamino attacks Sarastro's wickedness, but the Elderly Priest very quickly and convincingly persuades Tamino that he has been misled by a woman. Now confused, Tamino learns that the "unhappy woman, oppressed by great sorrow," is not to be trusted, or for that matter, no woman is to be trusted.

The Elderly Priest follows with a tirade condemning women, by modern standards, deplorable statements of male chauvinism: "Women do little and talk too much." It is Sarastro, at the close of Act I, who condemns the Queen before Pamina: "Only a man should guide women's hearts, because without man, every woman would stray."

And the Priests exhort Papageno in Act II - Scene 2: "Your first duty is to be aware of woman's treachery, because many men found themselves forsaken, led astray and ensnared by them"; all sentiments against women that were prevalent during the 18th century Enlightenment.

Tamino, previously convinced of Sarastro's evil and guilt, has become enlightened with new attitudes toward women. In Act II - Scene 2, after the Queen's Three Ladies try to arouse both Tamino and Papageno against Sarastro, Tamino repeats his new-found convictions when he warns Papageno not to listen to idle chatter spread by women and devised by hypocrites: "Women have repeated what bigots have invented!"

Freemasonry reached its flowering during the 18th century Enlightenment: both share many similar attitudes and ideologies toward women. The Enlightenment contained inferences and allusions of antifeminism, deeming woman's actions the antithesis of their ennobled reason, a capacity and gift that particularly belonged to males.

Mozart may have shared those Enlightenment attitudes, and even if he did not, he certainly delighted in portraying them in his operas. *Così fan tutte's* primary theme pontificates that women cannot be trusted: in *Don Giovanni,* Masetto complains about his fickle fiance, Zerlina; in the glorious duet from *Don Giovanni,* "Là ci darem la mano," Zerlina's "should I or shouldn't I" is saturated with female fickleness; and in *The Marriage of Figaro,* in Figaro's last-act aria, "Aprite un po' quell'occhi" ("Open your eyes a little"), he assures husbands emphatically that all wives are unfaithful.

The antifeminist diatribes of *The Magic Flute* seem to be echoes of fundamental ideologies of the Enlightenment, and likewise, those of Freemasonry. Yet metaphorically, *The Magic Flute's* antifeminism could very well be more specific to just one woman: it could represent a condemnation against a power-hungry and politically motivated woman; the Queen of the Night may be the operatic representation of the abusive Empress Maria Theresa of Austria, perceived to be the incarnation of arch evil by the oppressed Freemasons.

Nevertheless, from a dramatic point of view, to justify Tamino's transformation and change of allegiance after the admonishment from the Elderly Priest, the authors had to stress the basic unreliability of female credibility, an idea not too difficult during the Enlightenment. As a result, in *The Magic Flute* story, the Queen's allegations cannot be trusted and she is deemed a liar; as such, the story becomes endowed with an antifeminist or male chauvinist bias.

The rituals and ceremonies portrayed in *The Magic Flute* contain an aura of real mystery: all are associated with ancient Egyptian religious traditions that ultimately had become fundamental to Freemasonry.

About 3000 years ago, the son of Ramses I, Seti, (or Sethos), elevated the god Osiris, his wife Isis, and their child Horus, to the loftiest niches in the Egyptian pantheon of gods. At the end of Act II - Scene 1 of *The Magic Flute*, the fraternal order's solemn praise of Isis and Osiris is hauntingly depicted in a majestic and awe-inspiring chorus: "O, Isis und Osiris."

With respect to the "magic flute" instrument itself, according to legends, Osiris invented a flute that possessed supernatural powers. It became an integral accompaniment to mysterious ceremonial rites, but also possessed the power to subjugate nations and disarm enemies.

In ancient Egypt, life on earth was a stage in the passage toward a glorious afterlife: death, the hereafter, and reincarnation pervaded their spiritual world; Isis and Osiris were divine functionaries who accompanied deceased souls on their spiritual journey. As such, Isis and Osiris can be viewed as complementary or rhyming gods; symbols of regeneration and rebirth. In many respects, the ordeals that Pamina and Tamino face in their purification ritual represent an elevation of consciousness, but in a mythological interpretation, they also signify the idea of rebirth through union.

Three thousand years after Seti, during the 18th century Enlightenment, legends associated with his towering monuments and achievements captivated the imagination of the European mind: they stimulated a proliferation of books about Egypt, all of which contained imaginative visions of exotic landscapes, the flowing Nile, palm trees, sandy wastes, majestic pyramids, and most of all, arcane religious rituals.

One of the most popular novels about Egypt was *Sethos* (1731), by Abbé Jean Terrasson, a French professor of philosophy, which contained an account of Seti's education and initiation into the mysteries of ancient Egyptian religions. Although the work's authenticity became questioned and controversial, the author eventually became the accepted authority on ancient Egyptian religion, their initiation rites, as well as their underlying philosophies and ideologies. There are numerous incidents and characters in *The Magic Flute* which have counterparts in Terrasson's novel: there is no doubt that the authors of the opera libretto had more than a casual familiarity with the novel, as well as with those esoteric rituals and exotic symbolisms of Freemasonry, all of which were specifically derived from ancient Egyptian religious rites.

Freemasonry began its organized existence in the early 18th century in England, originally evolving from guilds of cathedral-building stonemasons from the Middle Ages; with the decline of cathedral building, lodges began to bolster membership by accepting honorary members. Very soon thereafter, Freemasonry spread quickly throughout Europe, all the lodges practicing their arcane religious rituals and symbolism largely from descriptions in Terrasson's popular novel, *Sethos*. By the mid-eighteenth century, Freemasonry had become a potent spiritual force in Europe.

The secrecy of Freemasonry rituals was in part their protection against powerful antagonists. From its inception, societies encountered considerable opposition from religious groups, in particular, the Roman Catholic Church, as well as from the ruling European monarchies and autocracies: all those opponents maintained their conviction that the French Revolution was fomented, at least in part, by Masonic lodges.

However, Freemasonry is not a religious institution, although it contains many essential elements of religion such as the belief in the existence of a Supreme Being, and in the immortality of the soul. Early Freemasons intended to propagate Enlightenment ideals: reason and wisdom, freedom, equality and justice, a strong advocacy of morality, charity, and obedience to the law of the land. Benjamin Franklin and Alexander Hamilton were Freemasons: neither they nor the ideas espoused in the new American Constitution endeared themselves to European monarchies. Nevertheless, Freemasonry has survived for two centuries: a Freemasonry group prevalent in the United States and known for their charitable work is the Ancient Order of the Nobles of the Mystic Shrine: the "Shriners."

At *The Magic Flute's* premiere, its theatrical presentation of Masonic secret rites was recognized immediately, igniting antagonism and controversy from both Freemasons as well as from their usual opponents, the Church and the autocracies.

In Austria, the practice of Freemasonry was discouraged, persecuted, and even outlawed. In 1742, the first Vienna lodge, "The Three Firing Glasses" was founded, and among its members was Francis of Lorraine, the husband of the then Archduchess Maria Theresa. It is rumored that she precipitated a raid on the lodge which obliged her husband to escape by the back stairs, nevertheless, the members — her husband included — continued to meet in secret. Two more lodges were founded in Austria by the time of her death, and four more during the reign of her more liberal son, Emperor Joseph II. In 1784, Mozart joined the Lodge *Zur Wohltatigkeit,* or the Lodge of Benevolence, eventually attaining the grade of master.

In addressing Masonic symbolism contained in *The Magic Flute*, and considering its suppression by Austrian authorities, the story's possible political associations endow it with much historical interest and curiosity: the characters may represent real historical personages disguised in their operatic alter egos.

The Queen of the Night has been compared to her royal counterpart, the Empress Maria Theresa. The Queen transforms from a good woman into a raging, avenging, and evil antagonist: likewise, the Empress Maria Theresa was initially deemed righteous and principled, but many Austrians believed that she later betrayed them. In 1791, the year of *The Magic Flute's* premiere, the Empress Maria Theresa had been dead for seven years, but her earlier actions to suppress Freemasonry were not forgotten: she was condemned posthumously.

The Empress dutifully shared the prevalent conviction that the French and American Revolutions were inspired by Freemasons. In fact, an official Viennese government memorandum expressed those sentiments and condemned the secret societies: "The defection of the English colonies in America was the first operation of this secret ruling elite . . . and there can be no doubt that the overthrow of the French Monarchy is the work of such a secret society." The Queen of the Night, who transforms into an angry, frustrated, and vindictive woman, is an operatic characterization uncannily close to that of the controversial Austrian Empress.

In contrast, Maria Theresa's son, Joseph II, openly protected the Masonic orders when he came to the throne: he was a man of noble character and has been likened to Prince Tamino.

The austere Sarastro was supposedly modeled after the Masonic scientist, Izgnaz von Born, an expert on the myths of Greece and Egypt, although he had parted with the Masons several years before *The Magic Flute* was written.

Pamina, in an allegorical sense, presumably represented Austria: she becomes enlightened by the wisdom of freemasonry, and rescues its people from the powerful, autocratic church.

Why would Schikaneder and Mozart, both Freemasons, choose to expropriate the Masonic secrecy they had sworn to uphold?

One hypothesis speculates that their public display of Masonic secrets emanated from their desires to enlighten the world about the benevolent nature of the order, and thus, they would combat the fierce hostility and opposition to their ideals. Another hypothesis speculates that at the time, Freemasonry was in decline, and most Austrian lodges had disbanded in response to official hostility: the authors may have considered any revelation of Masonry's secret rites to be insignificant.

Nevertheless, *The Magic Flute* indeed publicly reveals Masonic secret rites and symbols, as well as some of its profound philosophical ideology. As a result, *The Magic Flute's* revelations naturally offended other members of the Brotherhood, eventually inflaming bitterness and animosity that would hound Mozart to the grave and beyond.

The premiere of *The Magic Flute* took place on September 30, 1791, at Schikaneder's *Theater auf der Wieden.* Mozart himself conducted from the clavier, and Schikaneder played the role of the bird-catcher, Papageno. Very soon thereafter, the opera became an unqualified success. A few years afterwards, a resident of the area described his pursuit of an inexpensive ticket to a performance: it was necessary to arrive at the theater by mid-afternoon, and wait for three hours while being "bathed in heat and sweat and impregnated by the garlicky fumes of the smoked meats being consumed." Of all of Mozart's operas, *The Magic Flute* became his greatest popular success.

Just hours before he died, Mozart's wife, Constanze, had great difficulty persuading a cleric to perform the rites. The hesitation was no doubt caused by Mozart's openly avowed Masonic affinity, which he clearly engraved in *The Magic Flute's* text and music. In mid-November, two months after *The Magic Flute's* premiere, Mozart, depressed and ill, took to his bed and died.

The actual cause of Mozart's death remains a highly controversial subject in musical academia. The popular dramatic play, "Amadeus," posed the theory that Mozart died from a poison given to him by the court composer, Antonio Salieri, a fiction that has been thoroughly discredited by historical fact.

Another theory hypothesizes that his publicizing of Masonic rituals in *The Magic Flute* aroused so much enmity from fellow Masons that they murdered him in revenge. Another speculates that his rather harsh portrayal of the Queen of the Night, therefore, Maria Theresa, provoked a political assassination. And yet another, that his use of a Catholic Kyrie and a Lutheran hymn, both clothed in the finale's Masonic ceremony, were blasphemous, and thus provoked a death plot.

In 1936, Mathilde Ludendorff, wife of the Nazi general Erich Ludendorff, suggested that Mozart participated in a plot to rescue Marie-Antoinette from her captors, all allegedly Masons, which ultimately resulted in a fatal counterplot against him.

In recent years, these claims have all been proven to be absurd fantasies. Mozart's medical records have been examined by respected modern medical professionals, who have conclusively determined that he died from a streptococcal infection, renal failure, bronchopneumonia, and cerebral hemorrhage: there has been no evidence of poison.

The quality of *The Magic Flute's* libretto continues to spark controversy. The great English musicologist, Ernest Newman, writing in the 1920s, noted quite contentiously that "The greater part of the text is miserable hack work that would be within the powers of anyone who could handle a pen." Before him, the Mozart scholar Professor Edward J. Dent termed the libretto "one of the most absurd specimens of that form of literature in which absurdity is only too often a matter of course."

Contrarily, Goethe became so overwhelmed by *The Magic Flute's* folk elements and popular romanticism that he began to write a sequel in which his scenario had the Queen of the Night reappearing to rescue not Pamina, but Pamina's infant son: Sarastro abandons the order to journey across the earth as a nameless wanderer. Goethe's sequel remained a fragment, partly because no composer dared to risk composing it and thus be compared to Mozart. But Goethe's indulgence with *The Magic Flute* clearly indicates that the greatest intellectual of the century believed that *The Magic Flute's* story was far from absurd, and certainly was imbedded with profound insights into universal humanity.

The fairytale elements of *The Magic Flute* make a profound statement about the moralistic themes of right vs. wrong, and good vs. evil: good represents enduring virtues and qualities which benefit humanity; evil represents actions that are devoid of conscience or principle whose ambitions cannot be suppressed.

It is a magnificent moment of dramatic tension and conflict in Act II - Scene 3 when the Queen of the Night, seething with vengeance, forces a dagger into Pamina's hand and commands her to murder Sarastro. If Pamina should refuse, the Queen threatens to disown her: an unbearable curse. But Pamina stands, dagger in hand and without fear, courageously defending the principles of right, and refusing to commit murder.

One of *The Magic Flute's* underlying messages is that humanity can never abandon conscience: an inhumane, immoral, or evil act, cannot be justified in the name of obedience to a parent, or a command from a higher authority. It is a powerful message that alludes to universal conflicts involving man's duty to god, state, and humanity, and the inherent tension in which moral convictions must remain unyielding.

*T*he *Magic Flute's* story can be viewed in terms of mythological symbolism: it is an archetypal story representing man's progression from nature to culture, or from instinct to reason. The late Robert Donington, author of two impressive books which heavily rely on the discoveries of the 20th century psychiatrist Carl Jung, provided an illuminating interpretation of opera characterizations and stories from the point of view of conscious and unconscious mythological symbols: *Opera & Its Symbols* (1990), and earlier, (Wagner's) *The Ring and its Symbols* (1963).

Joseph Campbell's popular interpretations of mythology confirm that in all civilizations, myth reflects man's collective unconscious. In most myths, the hero embarks on an initiation into manhood and maturity: he breaks from his blissful state with mother (nature, the physical source of being), and seeks the father (wisdom, culture, discipline, and reason). In *The Magic Flute,* Tamino is the symbolic and archetypal young mythological hero: he embarks on an adventure that becomes his initiation into maturity; that classic synthesis of maternal love and paternal reason.

The hero traditionally encounters a fearsome female, often represented in the figure of the dragon: he is liberated when he slays the dragon — or Sphinx — and thus defeats that potentially destructive aspect of the female: he has destroyed the "Terrible Mother" image. In *The Magic Flute*, the serpent represents that fearsome female image to Tamino. He then encounters Sarastro and the Priests of Isis, his masculine archetypes who represent father figures, and therefore consciousness and wisdom.

Sarastro integrates Tamino's experiences. Tamino and Pamina pass through the initiation ordeals: fire, the archetypal male symbol; water, the archetypal female symbol; and finally, the hero and heroine arrive at maturity. It is significant that Pamina also experiences that same maturing process. At first, her world encompasses only her mother, the Queen of the Night, but as she is elevated to consciousness and awareness, she seeks wisdom from the father image.

The Queen of the Night represents that quintessential, ambivalent matriarch who appears to have been snatched right out of classical mythology and legend. Like all archetypes, she is ambivalent. At first she is despairing, sympathetic, and grieving, but then she transforms into a destructive, savage, vengeful, and evil woman. Pamina's mother represents the instinctive or intuitive aspects of nature, ambivalent elements which can be irrational: nature nurtures, but it also destroys; it can provide good as well as bad. In nature, reason is nonexistent, so Pamina, like Tamino, seek the father's wisdom and reason.

Sarastro, the archetypal benevolent and just father, is a name that is uncannily similar to the ancient Persian god Zoroaster: the god of eternal wisdom. Like all archetypal characters, Sarastro is ambivalent and therefore represents elements of both good and evil: he abducts Pamina because he deems that she is in need of enlightenment, and he subjects Pamina and Tamino to cruel and terrifying ordeals, because he is convinced that they serve a greater good.

Papageno, a "child of nature," also transforms from his carefree state of irresponsibility and protection from the mother — his employer, the Queen — to culture. Papageno also learns wisdom and reason, and is rewarded with a feminine counterpart, Papagena, his ultimate fulfillment.

Pamina and Tamino embark on their perilous ordeals into the swirling fires, and then into the rushing water. Textually and musically, they complement each other like Isis and Osiris, the ancient Egyptian gods of rebirth and regeneration. If Tamino must face death, Pamina will undergo the trial with him. In fact, she will lead him, ensuring their safe passage with the magic flute. Tamino and Pamina emerge from the trial unscathed, passing the supreme test of ritual purification by fire and water. With their transition and transformation complete, they have arrived at a new level of understanding: an archetypal journey from innocence to maturity, or, perhaps, in its counterpart, to a Masonic revelation of wisdom and enlightenment.

*T*he Magic Flute possesses Mozart's ingenious musical truthfulness: its noble music complements its story about man's spiritual growth, and his progress toward wisdom and light.

Mozart brilliantly used his music to truthfully portray character and circumstance: in *The Magic Flute,* he provided each character with a distinct and separate musical idiom; the Queen's music lies in the ornamental, high coloratura; Papageno's is almost folk-tunish; Tamino's, Italian and classical; and Pamina's, very German and romantic.

There is also a wonderful completeness, a marvelous lightness, a radiance, and a deceptive simplicity in the music: there is delicacy in Tamino's aria, "Dies Bildnis ist bezaub schön" ("No one has seen such magical beauty as in this portrait"), when he breathlessly addresses the portrait of Pamina and his passion for the beautiful girl becomes inflamed.

Sarastro's music is virtually unique in Mozart's canon: he seems to be communicating on a higher musical plane than ever before. George Bernard Shaw commented that Sarastro's music sounds so sacred and holy that it would seem to come from the mouth of God. Perhaps Mozart was composing in a new "Masonic style": his low bass, Sarastro, and indeed, the Brotherhood's ceremonial music, possess an unusual solemnity and depth; Mozart's musical language is clearly exalting Freemasonry's ideals and ideology.

In the glorious final scene, Mozart combines two distinct liturgical idioms: a Kyrie from the Catholic Mass that was popular in his times with a Lutheran chorale. The underlying music seems holy and divine, commensurate with the moving inscription inscribed on the pyramid; "Der, welcher wandert diese Strasse voll Beschwerden" ("He who pursues this path full of dangers, becomes purified by fire, water, air, and earth.") And it continues, "If he can overcome fear and death, he will rise to heaven. Thus purified, he then will be able to devote himself completely to Isis's mysteries."

*T*he Magic Flute has become one of the most popular operas in the repertory for over two centuries: it is a magical story possessing many arcane and exciting secrets, and a story whose characters have become household names.

The excitement of *The Magic Flute* story is that it possesses profound hidden meanings: it is a fairy tale emphasizing the moral struggle between good and evil; it is an allegory dealing with Freemasonry and its contemporary political struggles; and it is a mythological story possessing archetypal significance.

Mozart was a supreme musical dramatist who endowed *The Magic Flute* with his universally understood musical language: his music possesses a sublime power as it reaches deeply into the human soul and conscience. Like the journey to wisdom, reason and enlightenment, for Pamina and Tamino, *The Magic Flute* provides a sublime "magical" adventure as it elevates its listener to a transcendent world through Mozart's incandescent music, music of unrivalled beauty.

Principal Characters in The Magic Flute

Tamino, a Javanese prince	Tenor
Papageno, a birdcatcher, employed by the Queen of the Night	Baritone
The Queen of the Night	Coloratura soprano
Pamina, daughter of the Queen of the Night	Soprano
Sarastro, Priest of Isis and Osiris	Bass
Elderly Priest (also referred to as the Sprecher, Orator, or Speaker	Bass
Three Priests	Bass, Tenor, and Spoken
Monostatos, a Moor, overseer of the Temple	Tenor
Three Ladies, attendants of the Queen	2 Sopranos, Mezzo-soprano
Old Woman (later Papagena)	Soprano
Three Young Boys (the Spirits)	Sopranos (2) and Mezzo-Soprano
Two men in Armor	Tenor, Bass
Three Slaves	Spoken

Priests of the Temple of Isis,
attendants and slaves

TIME: Ancient Egypt, about the time of Ramses I

PLACE: Vicinity of the Temple of Isis and Osiris

Brief Story Synopsis

In the first act of *The Magic Flute,* Prince Tamino and his new-found friend, the birdcatcher Papageno, embark on their quest to rescue Pamina, the beautiful daughter of the Queen of the Night. Pamina was abducted by Sarastro, the High Priest of Isis and Osiris, Sarastro; his purpose was to separate Pamina from the evil influence of her mother. With the aid of a magic flute, Tamino rescues Pamina, and they fall in love.

In the second act, Tamino and Papageno enter a series of initiation trials into the secret order of Sarastro's temple: Tamino becomes inspired toward wisdom and enlightenment, and Papageno toward a wife for whom he yearns. Pamina misunderstands Tamino's duty-bound silence as rejection: Papageno, also duty-bound to silence, chatters incessantly and almost loses his new-found love, Papagena.

With the aid of the magic flute, Tamino and Pamina succeed in the order's ordeals: all have matured and discovered love and wisdom.

Story Narrative with Music Highlights

Overture:

An Adagio, solemn and somber, announces the *Dreimalige Akkord:* the "thrice played chord" that has been interpreted as a musical simulation of the three traditional knocks made by Freemasons on the door to their fraternal lodges. The mood is tranquil, yet it conveys a mysterious and supernatural ambience.

"Dreimalige Akkord"

A brilliant Allegro in fugue form repeats, weaves, and develops successive themes in breathtaking musical counterpoint.

ACT I - Scene 1: A forest area in the mountains. In the foreground, a cave, and in the background, the Temple of the Queen of the Night.

Tamino, a prince, appears, bearing a bow without arrow. He was separated from his traveling companions, and is now being pursued by a serpent. He is in fear and fright, cries out vainly for help, and then falls to the ground unconscious.

"Zu Hülfe! Zu Hüfle!"

Three Ladies, attendants to the Queen of the Night, suddenly appear and slay the serpent.

"Stirb, Ungeheur! durch unsre Macht!"

Stirb,   Un - ge - heur! durch uns - re Macht!
Die, you monster, our power will kill you!

The Three Ladies admire the handsome, unconscious youth: they fantasize that if they were permitted to love, they would dedicate themselves to him wholeheartedly. The Three Ladies decide to tell the Queen about this dashing young man: he might possibly aid her in resolving her present dilemma.

A delightfully comic quarrel develops between the Three Ladies, each insisting that she remain behind to protect the unconscious young prince. Nevertheless, they bid farewell to the prince, and yearn to see him again.

Prince Tamino awakens, dazed and bewildered, and wonders whether he is alive or dead: his anxieties dissolve when he notices the dead serpent at his feet. In the distance, he hears the sounds of a *Waldflötchen,* a forest-piccolo, and he hides behind a tree.

The music heralds the arrival of Papageno, the Queen of the Night's roguish bird-catcher and would-be ladies' man; he is feather-clad, and on his back he bears a large cage filled with birds. He brags boastfully about his occupation, but admits that he would much rather be catching pretty girls in his net than birds. Papageno, simple and innocent, is a charming child of nature: carefree, perky, quick-witted, and good-humored.

"Der Vogelfänger bin ich ja"

Der Vo - gel-fän - ger bin ich ja, stets lu - stig hei - sa hop-sa-sa!
I'm the birdcatcher, who's always happy! Hi ho!

Tamino emerges from hiding and converses with the quaint but outlandish looking stranger. At first, he seemingly insults him by claiming that he looks more like a bird than a human being. Papageno refutes him, claiming that he possesses a giant's strength; however, the sight of the dead serpent terrifies him. After he assures himself that the serpent is indeed dead, he boasts that he strangled the monster with his bare hands: graciously, Tamino thanks him for saving his life.

Tamino reveals that he is a prince, and Papageno explains that he catches birds for the mysterious "star-flaming" Queen and her Three Ladies, and that he is rewarded for his services daily with "wine, cake, and sweet figs." Tamino becomes excited, for he realizes that he is in the realm of the powerful Queen of the Night about whom his father had often spoken.

The Three Ladies reappear. They overheard Papageno's boastful lie about having killed the serpent, and in punishment, withhold his usual reward: they give him a bottle of water instead of wine, a stone instead of cake, and no sweet figs. Instead, they punish him by fastening his mouth with a padlock; Papageno is unable to speak, and his conversation is reduced to "Hm, hm, hm."

The Third Lady reveals to Tamino that she and her colleagues killed the serpent. Then she shows him a portrait of Pamina, the Queen of the Night's beautiful daughter. She explains that if he finds her engaging, happiness, honor, and fame will await him. After the Ladies depart, Tamino passionately rhapsodizes on the girl's beauty: his love for her intensifies and he vows to possess her.

"Dies Bildnis ist bezabernd schön"

Larghetto
TAMINO

Dies Bild - nis ist bezanbernd schön,   wie noch kein Au-ge je ge - sehn!
No one has ever seen such magical beauty as in this portrait!

As Tamino pledges eternal love to the beautiful girl in the portrait, a clap of thunder announces the arrival of the Queen of the Night. She has come to persuade Tamino to become her daughter's rescuer.

The sobbing Queen recreates the events of Pamina's abduction, a terrifying moment in which Pamina was cruelly kidnapped by the wicked Sarastro. She could only look on, because she was powerless to help her daughter. With resolution, the Queen suggests that Tamino rescue her daughter: if he succeeds, she will reward him with her daughter's hand in marriage.

The Queen expresses her despair and anguish in a dramatic explosion of passion in an energetic coloratura aria.

"Zum Leiden bin ich auserkoren"

Larghetto
QUEEN OF THE NIGHT

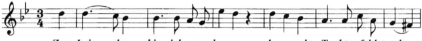

Zum Lei - den   bin ich auserkoren,   denn meine Tochter fehlet mir.
Since my daughter is gone, I have been doomed to suffer.

At the sound of a thunderclap, the Queen departs. Tamino becomes deeply moved by the Queen's despair.

Tamino agrees to undertake Pamina's rescue. To help him, the Three Ladies furnish him with a magic flute, explaining that when in danger, the sounds from the flute will protect its bearer and ensure his safety. Papageno is assigned to accompany Tamino. The Three Ladies remove the padlock from his lips, and sternly warn him about future lying: Papageno promises never to lie again.

The Three Ladies give Papageno a glockenspiel (chimes), whose magic power, like Tamino's flute, will protect him when in danger. After the Three Ladies depart, Tamino and Papageno set out on their mission, guided on their journey by Three Youths (The Three Boys or Three Spirits).

ACT I - Scene 2: A room in Sarastro's palace

Monostatos, a Moor serving Sarastro, has been assigned to guard Pamina: she is chained and unconscious, and Monostatos expresses his lust for her.

While the Moor remains entranced by the beautiful sleeping young maiden, he does not notice that Papageno has been watching him from a window. Papageno suddenly enters the room; they eye each other in shock and terror, each believing that the other is the devil. In fear, each flees in different directions.

After Papageno returns, Pamina awakens. Papageno becomes excited, realizing that he has found Pamina, the incarnation of the portrait, and therefore the Queen's daughter. But Pamina looks upon him with suspicion. Papageno ensures her trust by showing her the ribbon he wears around his neck, a symbol given to him by the Three Ladies to identify him.

Pamina and Papageno conspire to escape and seek the help of Tamino. Just before they depart, Pamina learns that Papageno has neither wife nor sweetheart: she compassionately consoles him, telling him about the virtues of love.

"Bei Männern, welche Liebe fühlen"

Andantino
PAMINA

Bei Männern, welche Lie - be fühlen, fehlt auch ein gu - tes Her - ze nicht.
Men who experience love, always possess a good heart.

ACT I - Scene 3: A grove. There are three temples, each bearing an inscription: Temple of Wisdom, Temple of Reason, and Temple of Nature.

The Three Boys lead Tamino to the grove that overlooks Sarastro's three temples: before they leave, they caution him to be steadfast, persevering, and silent.

Tamino expresses his resolve, warning the wicked sorcerer — Sarastro — that he is determined to free Pamina. He begins his search by striding to the door of the Temple of Reason. He opens the door and hears the stern voice of a priest from inside warning him not to enter. He then goes to the Temple of Wisdom, where the Elderly Priest advises him that Sarastro can be found inside the temple. Tamino, persuaded by the Queen that Sarastro is a wicked and evil man, condemns his hypocritical association with wisdom.

The Elderly Priest interrogates Tamino and discovers that his conviction that Sarastro is evil emanates from what he has been told by a woman. The Elderly Priest admonishes him about woman's treachery: "So a woman tricked you? Women do little and talk too much." Nevertheless, Tamino condemns Sarastro for what he believes was his unconscionable act of kidnapping Pamina from her mother. At the same time, Tamino becomes fearful that the young girl he has fallen in love with has perhaps become a sacrificial offering.

The Elderly Priest describes Sarastro's noble character to Tamino, explaining that he is a man of lofty ideals who governs their brotherhood with virtue and truth. Tamino sneers, reminding the Elderly Priest that abducting Pamina contradicts virtue. Apologetically, the Elderly Priest reveals that his duty forbids him to speak further: he is bound by an oath of silence which can only be broken "As soon as the hand of friendship leads you into the sanctuary of the sacred brotherhood."

After the Priest disappears inside the temple, Tamino becomes prey to his conflicting thoughts and emotions: he loves Pamina, although he has only seen her in her portrait, and he has pity for the Queen who has lost her daughter. Suddenly, Tamino becomes possessed to learn the truth: he yearns for wisdom and knowledge; he wants to learn about Sarastro and the brotherhood. With intense poignancy, Tamino prays that he may learn the truth.

Solemn and mysterious voices are heard from inside the temple, assuring Tamino that Pamina lives, and that he will soon learn the truth. Overjoyed and thankful, Tamino begins to play his flute. Suddenly, animals congregate to hear him, but when he stops, they run away. Tamino becomes frustrated: of all living creatures it seems that only Pamina remains unaffected by the magical tones of his flute. Tamino takes up his flute again, hoping that this time Pamina will heed his call: each time he plays, he only hears the distant echoes from his flute.

Then, seemingly answering his flute, Tamino hears Papageno's glockenspiel. Ecstatic that he has found his companion, he rushes off to greet him. However, the echoes from Papageno's glockenspiel have misled him, and he takes the wrong direction. He has scarcely left, when Pamina and Papageno arrive anxiously in search of Tamino.

Now Papageno plays his glockenspiel and hears an answer from Tamino's flute. Pamina and Papageno, delighted that they have discovered Tamino so near to them, set off to find him, but they are barred by Monostatos, who is sneering and gloating over his new-found captives: he calls for slaves to put Pamina and Papageno in chains.

Papageno has an inspired idea to overcome danger: he begins to play a tune on his glockenspiel. His music casts a spell on Monostatos and his slaves who become entranced, passive, and then erupt into song and dance.

Immensely relieved, Pamina and Papageno express their dream: it would be so wonderful if every one had a "magic" glockenspiel; not only would their enemies disappear, but all humanity would live happily and in harmony.

Just as Pamina and Papageno are about to set out again in search of Tamino, a fanfare of drums and trumpets herald the arrival of Sarastro, the High Priest of Isis, who makes a majestic entrance followed by a host of attendants and followers. Papageno panics and trembles with fear and fright: Pamina remains calm and advises Papageno that above all, they must be truthful to Sarastro.

Pamina kneels before Sarastro and confesses her guilt: "Lord, I am guilty, because I wished to flee from your power." But Pamina explains that the reason she fled was because the evil Monostatos lusted for her. With an aura of gentleness, dignity, wisdom, and benevolence, Sarastro comforts Pamina with assurances that he knows well her goodness and virtue. However, he advises her that she must remain with him for her own benefit: he will not reunite her with her mother because the Queen of the Night is a haughty woman who is possessed by evil. Gently and sentimentally, Pamina responds to Sarastro's mention of her mother: "The mention of my mother sounds so sweet to me." Sarastro immediately dismisses the subject of the Queen of the Night, and introduces Pamina to Tamino, who had also been captured by Monostatos and his Slaves.

Tamino and Pamina behold each other for the first time, but as they embrace rapturously, Monostatos separates them. Monostatos kneels before Sarastro, prides his cleverness and vigilance, and seeks a reward for capturing Tamino and Pamina.

Sarastro prescribes his reward: Monostatos is to be whipped. Monostatos complains, but Sarastro grimly responds that his duty compelled him to exact the punishment. As Monostatos is led away, Sarastro's followers praise their High Priest for his divine wisdom and judiciousness: he is a leader who rewards and punishes with impartiality.

Solemnly, Sarastro orders that Tamino and Papageno be veiled and begin their initiation rituals into the brotherhood: they are led to the temple to be purified by the secret rites of the order of Isis and Osiris.

Act II – Scene I: A palm grove in which all of the trees are silver, and their leaves are golden

In an awe-inspiring procession embedded with almost supernatural solemnity, Sarastro arrives with the Priests to praise their gods, Isis and Osiris.

"O Isis und Osiris"

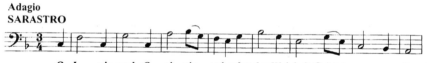

O I - sis und O - si - ris,   schenket der Weisheit Geist dem neu - en Paar!
Oh Isis and Osiris, lead this faithful pair to the path of wisdom!

Sarastro, the Elderly Priest, and other Priests, have assembled to consider whether Tamino is a worthy candidate for initiation into their order's austere mysteries. Sarastro reveals that the gods have ordained Tamino's marriage to Pamina, and assures his followers that the young prince possesses all of the order's attributes: he is virtuous, benevolent, and can maintain his silence. The Priests signify their acceptance and approval by blowing their horns three times: the *Dreimalige Akkord*.

Sarastro explains his reasons for abducting Pamina: "I kidnapped her from her haughty mother, who considers herself great. She hopes to beguile the populace through delusion and superstition, and to destroy the firm foundations of our temples." Sarastro emphasizes that if Tamino succeeds and becomes an initiate, he shall help them defend their noble ideals and punish wickedness in the world.

The Elderly Priest expresses his doubts whether Tamino, a prince, possesses the endurance necessary to survive the severity of the initiation ordeals, but Sarastro reaffirms his faith in Tamino. As the *Dreimalige Akkord* is sounded again, Tamino and Papageno are instructed about their responsibilities. Sarastro solemnly invokes Isis and Osiris, and begs the gods to grant wisdom, patience, strength, and guidance to the young initiates in their impending trials.

Act II - Scene 2: The courtyard of the Temple

It is a dark night, the menacing atmosphere accentuated by the sound of distant thunderclaps. Tamino and Papageno, their heads veiled, are advised by the Priests that their first test of endurance is silence: when Tamino beholds Pamina, he must not speak to her, and likewise, when Papageno sees Papagena, the beautiful bride who awaits him, he must also maintain silence. The Priests caution them that the most important rule of their fraternity is to beware the wiles of women: he who surrenders and falls into a woman's power, will wring his hands in vain.

Tamino and Papageno, their veils removed, are left alone in the darkness. Suddenly, torches herald the arrival of the Three Ladies, who become horrified when they discover that Tamino is being initiated into Sarastro's evil world, a betrayal of his vow to the Queen. They warn him that "those who join the brotherhood are doomed for life!"

The Three Ladies try to confound Tamino and Papageno, break their endurance, and tempt them to betray their oaths of silence. They succeed in cajoling Papageno, a natural chatter-box, who, fearing the Queen, loses his resistance and speaks. Tamino rebukes him for breaking his oath and admonishes him, explaining that the Queen is a woman, and as such, is not to be trusted. Bursts of thunder announce the arrival of Priests who immediately condemn the Three Ladies. In fear, they depart.

The Elderly Priest congratulates Tamino for successfully passing his first trial and maintaining his silence. Tamino and Papageno, their heads covered again, are led off to face their next ordeal.

Act II - Scene 3: A garden. Pamina sleeps, and the moon shines on her face.

Monostatos reflects on the harsh punishment he has received from Sarastro. He gazes at the sleeping Pamina and becomes smitten by her beauty. He laments his frustration at not being granted the pleasures of love.

"Alles fühlt der Liebe Freuden"

Allegro
MONOSTATOS

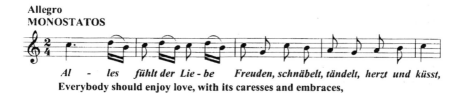

Al - les fühlt der Lie - be Freuden, schnäbelt, tändelt, herzt und küsst,
Everybody should enjoy love, with its caresses and embraces,

Monostatos approaches the sleeping Pamina and is about to kiss her when he becomes scared by a sudden roll of thunder. The Queen of the Night has arrived. She orders Monostatos away, and stands before Pamina.

The Queen imperiously explodes into a dramatic tirade about her obsession for revenge. Then, she commands Pamina that it is her duty to avenge her mother; if not, she will be disowned as her daughter.

The Queen, aware of her daughter's love for Tamino, advises her that she must persuade Tamino to escape from the evil brotherhood or he will be forever doomed. Pamina, confused and distraught, asks her mother why she bears such animosity toward the brotherhood. After all, her father was a member of the order, and he was a man of goodness, reason, and virtue.

The Queen explains that her father bore the order's all-powerful zodiac, the seven-sided sun shield that she willfully surrendered to Sarastro, the High Priest of the brotherhood, after her father's death. Without the zodiac, the Queen's power vanished.

The Queen reaffirms that Sarastro is her mortal enemy. She gives Pamina a dagger and orders her to kill Sarastro and retrieve the mighty zodiac. Pamina protests, and the Queen becomes inflamed, erupting into a vigorous fury, and defiantly calling for the vengeance of hell against Sarastro and the initiates.

"Der Hölle Rache kocht in meinem Herzen"

Allegro assai
QUEEN OF THE NIGHT

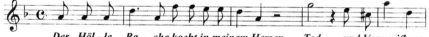

Der Höl-le Ra - che kocht in meinem Herzen,   Tod   und Verzweiflung,
The pangs of hell are raging in my bosom. Death and destruction,

After a roar of thunder, the Queen departs.

Pamina, alone, gazes in bewilderment at the dagger in her hand, and vows that she cannot and will not kill Sarastro. Monostatos approaches the anxious girl, seizes the dagger from her, and threatens that unless she yield to him, he will tell Sarastro that she and her mother are plotting to assassinate him. Pamina is terrified, but resolutely refuses to yield.

Just as the Moor is about to physically assault her, Sarastro suddenly appears and steps between them. Monostatos declares that Pamina was plotting to kill him, and proudly announces that he has saved his master's life. But the omniscient Sarastro well knows the Moor's wickedness and condemns him; Monastatos decides to seek revenge by joining forces with the Queen.

Pamina begs Sarastro not to punish her mother, and he relieves her fears by advising her that revenge is contrary to the teachings of their order: enemies receive forgiveness. Nevertheless, he assures her that ultimately the Queen's wickedness will be defeated by Tamino's courage and fortitude: Pamina's happiness with Tamino will injure the Queen's pride, forcing her to return to her castle in shame and defeat.

"In diesen heilgen Hallen kennt man die Rache nicht"

In die - sen heil - gen   Hallen kennt   man die   Ra - che   nicht,
Within these sacred walls, revenge and sorrow do not exist.

Act II - Scene 4: A Hall in the Temple of Probation

Tamino and Papageno await their next ordeal. Papageno, overcome with a craving thirst, cannot restrain himself from chattering with an old woman who bears a jug of water. The woman scares him by announcing that they are to be lovers. Just as she is about to reveal her name, a menacing roar of thunder frightens her away: the thunder reminds Papageno that he has vowed silence, and he swears he will not speak another word.

The Three Youths appear, bearing Tamino's flute and Papageno's glockenspiel. They prepare a lavish table laden with food and drink. Suddenly Pamina appears. She is overjoyed to have found Tamino and greets him rapturously. But Tamino — and Papageno — maintain their vows and remain silent. Confused and frustrated, Pamina begs to know the reason for Tamino's silence: she concludes that Tamino no longer loves her. Tamino gazes at Pamina sorrowfully while she pours out her grief and hopelessness. In her despair, she considers suicide..

"Ach, ich fuhl's es ist verschwunden"

Ach,ich fühl's es ist verschwunden,   e - wig   hin   mein ganzes Glück.
Oh, I feel that the happiness of love is gone forever!

Trumpets announce that Tamino and Papageno must proceed to the next phase of their initiation.

Act II - Scene 5: Interior vaults of the pyramid

Tamino, veiled again, appears before Sarastro and the Priests. Pamina is brought before them and is told to be patient: ultimately a happy outcome will befall both her and her lover. At the urging of Sarastro, the lovers bid each other farewell.

ACT II - Scene 6: A small garden

After all depart, Papageno arrives in search of Tamino, his thirst is so profound that he is prepared to renounce all hope of bliss for but one glass of wine. A large jug of wine magically appears from the ground. Papageno drinks the wine, recovers from his thirst, takes his glockenspiel, and accompanies himself in a song expressing his yearning for a wife.

"Ein Mädchen oder Weibchen wünscht Papageno sich"

Andante
PAPAGENO

Ein Mädchen o - der   Weib - chen   wünscht   Pa - pa - ge - no   sich,
A girl or a little wife is what Papageno would love to have!

The old woman reappears and threatens Papageno with a permanent diet of bread and water unless he swears eternal fidelity to her. After Papageno agrees, the old woman becomes transformed into Papagena, dressed identically in feathered clothes, and announcing that she is to become his coveted bride.

Just as he is about to embrace her, the Elderly Priest intervenes and gruffly sends Papagena away, telling her that Papageno is not yet worthy of her. Defying the Elderly Priest, Papageno tries to follow her, but suddenly the earth opens and Papageno is swallowed up.

The Three Youths appear and pray that the powers of light will overcome darkness.

"Bald prangt"
Andante
THREE YOUTHS

Bald prangt, den Morgen zu verkünden,   die   Sonn auf gold - ner   Bahn.
Soon the sun will rise to banish the night,

Just as they lament Pamina's suffering, she arrives, disconcerted and holding the dagger in her hand. In her distress and despair at having been spurned by Tamino, she poignantly addresses the dagger : it will be her bridegroom; a means to end her sorrow. As she raises the dagger to kill herself, the Three Youths intervene and explain that suicide is punishable by god. They reassure her that Tamino indeed loves her. Pamina rejoices and asks to be brought to Tamino.

Act II - Scene 7: Rugged cliffs at twilight. A huge iron gate stands between two mountains; on one side, a rushing and roaring stream, and on the other, a brightly glowing fire.

Men announce that those who are purified by fire, water, and air, shall be enlightened and devote themselves to the noble mysteries of Isis.

Pamina appears, and in a happy reunion with Tamino, the lovers embrace ardently. Pamina is deemed worthy to be ordained, and together, they are to begin purification and face the ordeal of fire and water. Pamina explains to Tamino that the magic flute will protect them in danger; her father fashioned it from a thousand-year-old oak and endowed it with magical powers.

Tamino plays the flute while they pass through the fiery cave. They emerge unscathed.

They proceed to the cave of rushing water; Tamino again plays his flute, and they emerge unharmed. The lovers thank the gods, and a chorus of Priests hail them as new initiates to be consecrated to Isis.

Act II - Scene 8: A garden

Papageno, now rescued after have fallen into the earth, searches for Papagena: in his sorrow at his loss, he decides to hang himself. Just as he ties a rope to a tree, the Three Youths arrive, scold and chide him for his rashness, and suggest that he play his magic glockenspiel to help find Papagena. After he plays the glockenspiel, Papagena appears: the couple explode in their joyous reunion, realizing that their destiny is to share a happy future together.

Act II - Scene 9: Rugged cliffs outside Sarastro's palace

Monostatos, the Queen of the Night, and the Three Ladies, bearing torches in the dark night, move stealthily toward Sarastro's temple. They are conspiring to break into the Temple and destroy Sarastro. Monostatos confirms that the Queen has promised Pamina as a reward for his help. Suddenly a storm erupts, with thunder, lightning, and the roar of gushing water. The earth opens, and all the villainous conspirators disappear.

Act II - Scene 10: The Temple of the Sun

Sarastro presides over a solemn assembly of Priests. Tamino and Pamina, both dressed in priestly robes, appear before them.

Majestically, Sarastro announces that Tamino and Pamina have succeeded in their trials and have become purified; they are now worthy to be consecrated to the worship of Isis and Osiris. The celebrants raise their voices in homage: "The strong have conquered, and as their reward, they are crowned with eternal beauty and wisdom."

The powers of darkness and evil have been destroyed by the noble ideals of reason and wisdom.

Libretto

THE MAGIC FLUTE

ACT I - Scene 1

A rocky, rugged cliff setting. Tamino, dressed in hunting clothes, appears with a bow but no arrows. He is being pursued by a serpent.

Allegro
TAMINO

Zu   Hül - fe!   zu Hül - fe!   Sonst bin   ich   ver - lo - ren!

TAMINO:
Zu Hülfe! Zu Hülfe! Sonst bin ich verloren,
der listigen Schlange zum Opfer erkoren.
Barmherzige Götter! Schon nahet sie sich!
Ach, rettet mich! Ach, schützet mich!

TAMINO:
Help! Help! Otherwise I'm lost, and I'll
become a victim of the cunning serpent.
Merciful Gods! It's already getting closer.
Oh, save me! Oh, protect me!

*Exhausted, Tamino falls down and becomes unconscious.
Three veiled ladies appear, carrying silver darts.*

Allegro
THREE LADIES

Stirb,   Un - ge - heur! durch uns - re   Macht!

DREI DAMEN:
Stirb, Ungeheur! Durch unsre Macht!

THE LADIES:
Die, you monster, our power will kill you!

(The Three Ladies kill the serpent.)

Triumph! Triumph! Sie ist vollbracht,
die Heldentat! Er ist befreit durch unsres
Armes Tapferkeit.

We did it! We did it! We accomplished an
heroic deed! He has been saved by our
courage.

ERSTE DAME:
Ein holder Jüngling, sanft und schön!

FIRST LADY: *(looking at Tamino)*
What a noble, gentle, handsome young man!

ZWEITE DAME:
So schön, als ich noch nie gesehn!

SECOND LADY:
I've never seen such a handsome man!

DRITTE DAME:
Ja, ja, gewiß zum Malen schön!

DREI DAMEN:
Würd' ich mein Herz der Liebe weihn,
so müßt es dieser Jüngling sein.
Laßt uns zu uns'rer Fürstin eilen,
ihr diese Nachricht zu erteilen.
Vielleicht daß dieser schöne Mann
die vor'ge Ruh' ihr geben kann.

ERSTE DAME:
So geht und sagt es ihr,
ich bleib indessen hier.

ZWEITE DAME:
Nein, nein, geht ihr nur hin,
ich wache hier für ihn!

DRITTE DAME:
Nein, nein, das kann nicht sein!
Ich schütze ihn allein.

ERSTE DAME:
Ich bleib' indessen hier!

ZWEITE DAME:
Ich wache hier für ihn!

DRITTE DAME:
Ich schütze ihn allein!

ERSTE DAME:
Ich bleibe!

ZWEITE DAME:
Ich wache!

DRITTE DAME:
Ich schütze!

DREI DAMEN:
Ich! Ich! Ich!
Ich sollte fort? Ei, ei, wie fein!
Sie wären gern bei ihm allein.
Nein, nein! Das kann nicht sein!

THIRD LADY:
He's handsome enough to be painted!

ALL:
If I would give my heart away
it would be to this young man.
Let's hurry to our Queen and tell her about
this news.
Maybe this handsome man can calm her
anxiety.

FIRST LADY:
So go and tell her. In the meantime I'm
staying here.

SECOND LADY:
No, no, you go,
I'll watch over him!

THIRD LADY:
No, no, that can't be! I'll protect him
myself.

FIRST LADY:
I'll stay here in the meantime!

SECOND LADY:
I'll watch over him!

THIRD LADY:
I'll protect him!

FIRST LADY:
I'll stay!

SECOND LADY:
I'll watch!

THIRD LADY:
I'll protect him!

THREE LADIES: (*each to themselves*)
I! I! I!
I should leave? Ha, ha, great!
She would love to be alone with him.
No, no! That can't be!

(each by themselves and then together)

Was wollte ich darum nicht geben,	What I wouldn't give if I could live with
könnt' ich mit diesem Jüngling leben!	this young man!
Hätt' ich ihn doch so ganz allein!	If I only I had him all to myself!
Doch keine geht; es kann nicht sein,	But that can't be, they're not leaving.
am besten ist es nun, ich geh'.	Therefore, it's best that I leave now.
	(to Tamino)
Du Jüngling, schön und liebevoll,	You handsome and lovable young man,
du trauter Jüngling, lebe wohl,	farewell till I see you again.
bis ich dich wiederseh'.	

The Three Ladies leave. Tamino awakens and looks around him fearfully.

TAMINO:

Wo bin ich? Ist's Fantasie, daß ich noch lebe? Oder hat eine höhere Macht mich gerettet?

Wie? Die bösartige Schlange ist tot?

Was hör ich? Ha, eine männliche Figur nähert sich.

TAMINO:

Where am I? Am I really still alive or did a higher power save me?

(He gets up and looks around)
What? That evil serpent is dead?

(The sound of a flute is heard in the distance.)
What do I hear? Oh, I see a man approaching.

Tamino hides behind a tree. Papageno arrives, dressed in feathers.
He carries a large bird cage on his back that is filled with various birds.
In his hands he holds a small flute.

Andante
PAPAGENO

Der Vo - gel-fän - ger bin ich ja, stets lu - stig hei - sa hop-sa-sa!

PAPAGENO:

Der Vogelfänger bin ich ja,
stets lustig, heisa, hopsasa!
Ich Vogelfänger bin bekannt
bei Alt und Jung im ganzen Land.
Weiß mit dem Locken umzugehn
und mich auf's Pfeifen zu verstehn.
Drum kann ich froh und lustig sein,
denn alle Vögel sind ja mein.

PAPAGENO:

I'm the bird-catcher, who's always happy!
Hi ho!
I'm known all over by young and old.
I know how to whistle every sound,
and I know all the birdcalls.
That's why I can be merry and happy,
because all the birds are mine.

Der Vogelfänger bin ich ja,
stets lustig, heisa, hopsassa!
Ich Vogelfänger bin bekannt
bei Alt und Jung im ganzen Land.

Ein Netz für Mädchen möchte ich,
ich fing sie dutzendweis für mich.
Dann sperrte ich sie bei mir ein,
und alle Mädchen wären mein.

Wenn alle Mädchen wären mein,
so tauschte ich brav Zucker ein.
Die, welche mir am liebsten wär',
der gäb' ich gleich den Zucker her.
Und küßte sie mich zärtlich dann,
wär' sie mein Weib und ich ihr Mann.
Sie schlief' an meiner Seite ein,
ich wiegte wie ein Kind sie ein.

I'm the bird-catcher, who's always happy!
Hi ho!
I'm known all over by young and old.

I'd like to have a net to catch girls by the
dozens.
I would lock them safely at home so that
they'd all be mine.

When they'd be mine, I'd give them sugar,
but I'd give sugar right away to the one I
love most.

Then if she would kiss me tenderly, it
would be as if we were husband and wife.
She would sleep beside me, and I would
rock her like a baby.

As Papageno blows his flute and begins to leave,
Tamino emerges from behind the tree where he was hiding.

TAMINO:
He da!

TAMINO:
Hey you!!

PAPAGENO:
Was da?

PAPAGENO:
What's that?

TAMINO:
Sag mir, du lustiger Freund, wer du seist?

TAMINO:
Tell me who you are, jolly friend?

PAPAGENO:
Wer ich bin? Dumme Frage!

Ein Mensch, wie du. Und wenn ich dich
nun fragte, wer du bist?

PAPAGENO: *(to himself)*
Who I am? What a stupid question!
(aloud)
I'm a man just like you. And what if I asked
you who you are?

TAMINO:
So würde ich dir antworten, daß ich aus
fürstlichem Geblüte bin.

TAMINO:
I would answer you, that I come from
royal ancestry.

PAPAGENO:
Das ist mir zu hoch. Mußt dich deutlicher
erklären, wenn ich dich verstehen soll!

PAPAGENO:
That's too complicated. You have to
explain that better in order for me to
understand you.

TAMINO:
Mein Vater ist ein Fürst, der über viele Länder und Menschen herrscht; darum nennt man mich Prinz.

PAPAGENO:
Länder? Menschen? Prinz? Sagst du mir zuvor: gibt's außer diesen Bergen auch noch Länder und Menschen?

TAMINO:
Viele Tausende!

PAPAGENO:
Da ließe sich ja eine Spekulation mit meinen Vögeln machen.

TAMINO:
Aber wie nennt man eigentlich diese Gegend? Und wer beherrscht sie?

PAPAGENO:
Das kann ich dir ebensowenig beantworten, als ich weiß, wie ich auf die Welt gekommen bin.

TAMINO:
Wie? Du wüßtest nicht, wo du geboren, oder wer deine Eltern waren?

PAPAGENO:
Kein Wort! Ich weiß nur so viel, daß nicht weit von hier meine Strohhütte steht, die mich vor Regen und Kälte schützt.

TAMINO:
Aber wie lebst du?

PAPAGENO:
Na, von Essen und Trinken, wie alle Menschen.

TAMINO:
Wodurch erhältst du das?

TAMINO:
My father is a king who rules many lands and peoples. That's why I'm called a prince.

PAPAGENO:
Many lands? People? Prince? Are you telling me that besides these mountains, other lands and peoples exist?

TAMINO:
Many thousands!

PAPAGENO:
My birds can figure that out.

TAMINO:
Tell me, what is this area called, and who rules it?

PAPAGENO:
I can't tell you that, just as I don't know how I came into this world.

TAMINO: *(laughs)*
What? You don't know where you were born and who your parents were?

PAPAGENO:
Quiet! I only know this much: that my straw cottage, which isn't far from here, protects me from the rain and cold.

TAMINO:
But how do you live?

PAPAGENO:
Just like everybody, from food and drink.

TAMINO:
How do you get that?

PAPAGENO:
Durch Tausch. Ich fange für die
sternflammende Königin und ihre Jungfrauen
verschiedene Vögel; dafür erhalte ich täglich
Speise und Trank von ihr.

PAPAGENO:
By trading. I catch various birds for the
star-flaming Queen and her young ladies,
and in exchange, I get my daily food and
drink.

TAMINO:
Sternflammende Königin? Wenn es etwa
gar die mächtige Herrscherin der Nacht
wäre! Sag mir, guter Freund, warst du
schon so glücklich, diese Göttin der Nacht
zu sehen?

TAMINO:
Star-flaming Queen? If only she would be
the almighty ruler of the night! Tell me,
good friend, were you ever fortunate
enough to see this goddess of the night?

PAPAGENO:
Sehen? Die sternflammende Königin
sehen? Welcher Sterbliche könnte sich
rühmen, die je gesehn zu haben?

PAPAGENO:
To see her? To see the star-flaming Queen?
What earthly mortal could boast to have
ever seen her?

TAMINO:
Nun ist's klar; es ist eben diese nächtliche
Königin, von der mein Vater mir so oft
erzählte. Unfehlbar ist auch dieser Mann
kein gewöhnlicher Mensch.

TAMINO: *(to himself)*
Now I understand. It is this Queen of the
Night that my father so often spoke to me
about. Undoubtedly, this man also is no
ordinary person.

PAPAGENO:
Wie er mich so starr anblickt!
Bald fang' ich an, mich vor ihm zu fürchten.

Warum siehst du so verdächtig und
schelmisch nach mir?

PAPAGENO: *(to himself)*
How he stares at me!
Soon I'll start to become afraid of him.
(aloud)
Why do you look at me so slyly and
suspiciously?

TAMINO:
Weil... weil ich zweifle ob du ein Mensch
bist.

TAMINO:
Because...because I doubt whether you're a
real human being.

PAPAGENO:
Wie war das?

PAPAGENO:
What did you say?

TAMINO:
Nach deinen Federn, die dich bedecken,
halt' ich dich...

TAMINO:
According to all those feathers covering
you, I think you're...

(Tamino approaches Papageno)

PAPAGENO:
Doch für keinen Vogel? Du, bleib zurück,
sag' ich, und traue mir nicht; denn ich habe
Riesenkraft.

Wenn er sich nicht bald von mir schrecken
lässt, so lauf ich davon.

TAMINO:
Riesenkraft?

Also warst du wohl gar mein Erretter, der
diese giftige Schlange bekämpfte?

PAPAGENO:
Schlange!

Ah! Ah! Ist sie tot oder lebendig?

TAMINO:
Aber um alles in der Welt, Freund, wie hast
du dieses Ungeheuer bekämpft? Du bist
ohne Waffen.

PAPAGENO:
Brauch keine! Bei mir ist ein starker Druck
mit der Hand mehr als Waffen.

TAMINO:
Du hast sie also erdrosselt?

PAPAGENO:
Erdrosselt!
Bin in meinem Leben nicht so stark
gewesen, als heute.

PAPAGENO:
Not a bird, I hope? I'm telling you, stay
back, and don't trust me, because I have
gigantic strength.
(to himself)
If I don't scare him off soon, then I'll
leave.

TAMINO:
Gigantic strength?
(He looks at the serpent.)
So it was you who rescued me by fighting
this poisonous serpent?

PAPAGENO:
Serpent?
(He looks around and trembles)
Is it dead or alive?

TAMINO:
My friend, how on earth did you conquer
this monster? You have no weapons!

PAPAGENO:
I don't need any! My strong hands are
better than weapons.

TAMINO:
So you strangled it?

PAPAGENO:
Strangled! *(to himself)*
In my life, I've never been as strong as I
am today.

*The Three Ladies appear, wearing veils. The First Lady carries an urn with water, the
second a stone, and the third a padlock and a medallion containing portrait.*

DREI DAMEN:

Papageno!

PAPAGENO:
Aha, das geht mich an!
Sieh dich um, freund.

THE THREE LADIES:
(threatening and shouting in unison)
Papageno!

PAPAGENO:
Oh, they're calling me! *(to Tamino)*
Look around, friend.

TAMINO:
Wer sind diese Damen?

PAPAGENO:
Wer sie eigentlich sind, weiß ich selbst nicht.
Ich weiß nur so viel, daß sie mir täglich meine
Vögel abnehmen, und mir dafür Wein,
Zuckerbrot und süße Feigen bringen.

TAMINO:
Sie sind vermutlich sehr schön?

PAPAGENO:
Ich denke nicht! Denn wann die schön
wären, dann würden die noch nicht ihre
Gesichter bedecken.

DREI DAMEN:
Papageno!

PAPAGENO:
Sei still! Sie drohen mir schon.

Ah, du fragst, ob sie schön sind, da kann
ich dir nichts anderes darauf antworten, als
daß ich in meinem Leben nichts
reizenderes gesehen habe.
Jetzt werd ich gleich wieder gut sein.

DREI DAMEN:
Papageno!

PAPAGENO:
Was hab ich bloß heute verbrochen, daß die
so aufgebracht wider mich sind?
Hier, meine Schönen, übergeb ich euch
meine Vögel.

ERSTE DAME:

Dafür schickt dir unsere Fürstin heute zum
ersten Mal statt Wein reines, helles Wasser.

TAMINO:
Who are these ladies?

PAPAGENO:
I really don't know who they are.
I only know that everyday they take my
birds from me, and in exchange, give me
wine, cake, and sweet figs.

TAMINO:
Do you think they're very beautiful?

PAPAGENO:
I do not think so, because if they were
beautiful they wouldn't cover their faces.

THE THREE LADIES: *(threatening)*
Papageno!

PAPAGENO: *(aside to Tamino)*
Be quiet! They're threatening me already.
(aloud)
Oh, you asked if they're beautiful. I can
only tell you that in my whole life, I've
never seen such beauties.
(to himself)
Now I'll behave myself again.

THREE LADIES:
Papageno!

PAPAGENO:
What in the world did I do wrong today to
provoke them?
Here, lovely ladies, here are my birds.

FIRST LADY:
(Gives Papageno the urn with water)
In return, today our princess sends you
clear water instead of wine.

ZWEITE DAME:
Und mir befahl sie, daß ich, statt
Zuckerbrot, diesen Stein dir überbringen
soll. Ich wünsche, daß er dir wohl
bekommen möge.

SECOND LADY:
And I was ordered to give you this stone
instead of cake. I hope you'll enjoy it.

PAPAGENO:
Was? Steine soll ich fressen?

PAPAGENO:
What? I have to eat stones now?

DRITTE DAME:
Und statt der süßen Feigen, hab' ich die
Ehre, dir dies goldene Schloß vor den
Mund zu schlagen.

THIRD LADY:
And I have the honor, instead of sweet figs,
to secure this golden padlock on your
mouth.

ERSTE DAME:
Du willst vermutlich wissen, warum die
Fürstin dich heute so wunderbar bestraft?

FIRST LADY:
You undoubtedly want to know why the
Queen is punishing you so wonderfully today?

(Papageno agrees by nodding his head)

ZWEITE DAME:
Damit du künftig nie mehr Fremde belügst.

SECOND LADY:
So that in the future you don't tell any
more lies to strangers.

DRITTE DAME:
Und daß du nie dich der Heldentaten
rühmst, die andre vollzogen haben.

THIRD LADY:
And that you'll never again take credit for
heroic deeds performed by others.

ERSTE DAME:
Sag an! Hast du diese Schlange bekämpft?

FIRST LADY:
Tell me! Did you fight this serpent?

(Papageno shakes no with his head)

ZWEITE DAME:
Wer denn also?

SECOND LADY:
Well who did it then?

(Papageno indicates that he doesn't know)

THIRD LADY:
Wir waren's, Jüngling, die dich befreiten.
Hier, dies Gemälde schickt dir die große
Fürstin; es ist das Bildnis ihrer Tochter.
"Findest du," sagte sie, "daß diese Züge dir
nicht gleichgültig sind, dann ist Glück, Ehr'
und Ruhm dein Los! Auf Wiedersehen.

THIRD LADY: *(to Tamino)*
Young man, we were the ones who rescued
you. Here, the great Queen sends you this
picture. It is a portrait of her daughter. She
said that if you like what you see,
happiness, honor, and fame will be yours!
Farewell!

ZWEITE DAME:
Adieu, Monsieur Papageno!

SECOND LADY:
Goodbye, Mr. Papageno!
(The Second and Third Ladies take the birdcage and leave)

ERSTE DAME:
Fein nicht zu hastig getrunken!

FIRST LADY:
He didn't drink that so quickly!
(The First Lady leaves laughing)

Papageno hastens away in dumb astonishment.
Tamino becomes captivated by the portrait, and his love becomes intensified.

Larghetto
TAMINO

Dies Bild - nis ist bezanbernd schön,   wie noch kein Au-ge je ge - sehn!

TAMINO:
Dies Bildnis ist bezanbernd schön,
wie noch kein Auge je gesehn!
Ich fühl es, wie dies Götterbild
mein Herz mit neuer Regung füllt.

Dies Etwas kann ich zwar nicht nennen,
doch fühl' ich's hier wie Feuer brennen.
Soll die Empfindung Liebe sein?
Ja, ja die Liebe ist's allein.

O wenn ich sie nur finden könnte!
O wenn sie doch schon vor mir stände!
Ich würde, würde, warm und rein.
Was würde ich?
Ich würde sie voll Entzücken
an diesen heißen Busen drücken,
und ewig wäre sie dann mein!

TAMINO:
No one has ever seen such magical beauty
as in this portrait!
As I look at this divine picture, my heart
beats excitedly.

I don't know what to call this feeling,
but its like a fire burning inside of me.
Is this what love feels like?
Yes, yes, this can only be love.

Oh, if I could only find her!
Oh, if she were already here!
Then I would be faithful and true.
What would I do?
I would charm her, and hold her against my
warm heart, and she would be mine
forever!

As it grows dark, there is a short, loud clap of thunder.
Tamino wants to leave, but the Three Ladies reappear.

Ihr Götter! Was ist das?   Good God! What is that?

ERSTE DAME:
Rüste dich mit Mut und Standhaftigkeit,
schöner Jüngling!
Die Fürstin....

ZWEITE DAME:
... hat mir aufgetragen, dir zu sagen...

DRITTE DAME:
daß der Weg zu deinem künftigen Glücke
nunmehr gebahnt sei.

ERSTE DAME:
Sie hat jedes deiner Worte gehört; Sie hat...

ZWEITE DAME:
...jeden Zug in deinem Gesichte gelesen...

DRITTE DAME:
...hat beschlossen, dich ganz glücklich zu
machen.

ERSTE DAME:
"Hat dieser Jüngling," sprach sie, "auch so
viel Mut und Tapferkeit, als er zärtlich ist, O,
so ist meine Tochter ganz gewiß gerettet."

TAMINO:
Gerettet?

ERSTE DAME:
Ein mächtiger, böser Dämon hat sie ihr
entrissen.

TAMINO:
Entrissen?
Sagt, sagt, wo ist des Tyrannen aufenthalt?

ZWEITE DAME:
Sehr nahe an unsern Bergen. Seine Burg ist
sorgsam bewacht.

TAMINO:
Pamina sei gerettet! Das schwör' ich bei
meiner Liebe, bei meinem Herzen.

FIRST LADY:
Prepare yourself with courage and
steadfastness, handsome young man!
The Queen...

SECOND LADY:
...has ordered me to tell you...

THIRD LADY:
that from now on, the road to your
future happiness is paved.

FIRST LADY:
She has heard every word you said, and she
has....

SECOND LADY:
...read every feature in your face...

THIRD LADY:
...and has decided to make you very happy.

FIRST LADY:
The Queen said: "if this young man has as
much courage and bravery as he is tender, oh,
then my daughter will definitely be rescued."

TAMINO:
Rescued?

FIRST LADY:
She was kidnapped by a strong and angry
demon.

TAMINO:
Kidnapped?
Tell me, where does this tyrant live?

THIRD LADY:
Very near our mountains. His fortress is
cautiously guarded.

TAMINO:
Pamina will be rescued! I swear it by my
heart and by my love.

Ihr Götter, was ist das?

(Short thunderclaps are heard)
Oh God, what is that?

DIE DREI DAMEN:
Fasse dich!

THE THREE LADIES:
Be calm!

ERSTE DAME:
Es verkündigt die Ankunft unserer
Königin.

FIRST LADY:
It announces the arrival of our Queen.

(Thunder roars)
DREI DAMEN:
Sie kommt! Sie kommt! Sie kommt!

THREE LADIES:
She's coming! She's coming! She's coming!

Amidst the stars in the sky, the Queen of the Night appears.

KÖNIGIN DER NACHT:
O zittre nicht, mein lieber Sohn!
Du bist unschuldig, weise, fromm;
Ein Jüngling so wie du vermag am besten,
Dies tiefbetrübte Mutterherz zu trösten.

QUEEN OF THE NIGHT:
Oh don't be frightened, beloved son!
You are innocent, devout and wise.
A young man like you surely knows how to
comfort this deeply saddened mother's heart.

Larghetto
QUEEN OF THE NIGHT

Zum Lei - den bin ich auserkoren, denn meine Tochter fehlet mir.

Zum Leiden bin ich auserkoren,
denn meine Tochter fehlet mir;
durch sie ging all mein Glück verloren,
ein Bösewicht entfloh mit ihr.
Noch seh ich ihr Zittern Mit bangem
Erschüttern, ihr ängstliches Beben,
ihr schüchternes Streben. Ich mußte sie mir
rauben sehen,
Ach helft! ach helft! war alles, was sie
sprach. Allein vergebens war ihr Flehen,
Denn meine Hilfe war zu schwach.

I have been doomed to suffer, and all of my
happiness has disappeared since my
daughter was kidnapped.
As a scoundrel abducted her, I still see her
shiver, tremble, and quiver, with no
strength to resist.

As I watched her being kidnapped, all she said
was oh help me, oh help me. Her pleading was all
in vain, since I was too weak to help her.

Du, du, du wirst sie zu befreien gehen,
Du wirst der Tochter Retter sein.
Und werd' ich dich als Sieger sehen,
So sei sie dann auf ewig dein.

You, you, you will go and rescue her.
You will be the rescuer of my daughter.
And if you succeed, she will be yours
forever.

As thunder roars, the Queen and the Three Ladies disappear.

TAMINO:
Ist's denn auch Wirklichkeit, was ich sah?
O ihr guten Götter, täuscht mich nicht!

PAPAGENO:

Hm, hm, hm, hm, hm!

TAMINO:
Der Arme kann von Strafe sagen, denn
seine Sprache ist dahin.

PAPAGENO:
Hm, hm, hm, hm, hm, hm!

TAMINO:
Ich kann nichts tun, als dich beklagen,
weil ich zu schwach zu helfen bin.

PAPAGENO:
Hm! Hm! Hm! Hm! Hm! Hm! Hm!

TAMINO:
Was that real?
Oh dear God, don't deceive me!

PAPAGENO:
(pointing sadly at the padlock on his mouth)
Hm, hm, hm, hm, hm, hm!

TAMINO:
The poor man was guilty of lying, and as a
penalty he can't talk anymore.

PAPAGENO:
Hm! hm! hm! hm! hm! hm! hm!

TAMINO:
I can't do anything but sympathize with
you, because I'm powerless to help you.

PAPAGENO:
Hm! Hhm! Hm! Hm! Hm! Hm! Hm!

The Three Ladies reappear. The First Lady carries a flute and chimes.

ERSTE DAME:
Die Königin begnadigt dich,
erläßt die Strafe dir durch mich.

THE FIRST LADY: *(to Papageno)*
I bring you the Queen's forgivenes and
pardon..

(She takes the padlock from his mouth)

PAPAGENO:
Nun plaudert Papageno wieder!

PAPAGENO:
Now Papageno can chatter again!

ZWEITE DAME:
Ja, plaudert! Lüge nur nicht wieder!

SECOND LADY:
Yes, chatter! But never lie again!

PAPAGENO:
Ich lüge nimmer mehr, nein, nein!

PAPAGENO:
I'll never lie again, not ever!

DREI DAMEN:
Dies Schloß soll deine Warnung sein.

THREE LADIES:
Let this padlock be your warning!

PAPAGENO:
Dies Schloß soll meine Warnung sein.

PAPAGENO:
This padlock shall be my warning.

ALLE:
Bekämen doch die Lügner alle
ein solches Schloß vor ihren Mund;
statt Haß, Verleumdung, schwarzer Galle,
bestünden Lieb' und Bruderbund.

ALL:
If only all liars would get such a lock on
their mouths, then we would have love and
friendship instead of hate and slander.

ERSTE DAME

O Prinz, nimm dies Geschenk von mir!
Dies sendet uns're Fürstin dir.
Die Zauberflöte wird dich schützen,
im größten Unglück unterstützen.

FIRST LADY:
(gives Tamino a golden flute)
Oh Prince, take this gift from me! Our
Queen commanded us to give it to you. This
Magic Flute will protect you in danger and
support you in your deepest sorrow.

DREI DAMEN:
Hiermit kannst du allmächtig handeln,
der Menschen Leidenschaft verwandeln:
der Traurige wird freudig sein,
den Hagestolz nimmt Liebe ein.

THE THREE LADIES:
With this flute you will possess divine powers.
You can reverse human suffering, convert
sadness to happiness, and assure that the
loveless will always be loved.

ALLE:
O so eine Flöte ist mehr als Gold und Kronen
wert, denn durch sie wird Menschenglück und
Zufriedenheit vermehrt.

ALL:
Oh, such a flute is worth its weight in gold,
because it brings untold happiness and
contentment to humanity.

PAPAGENO:
Nun, ihr schönen Frauenzimmer,
darf ich, so empfehl' ich mich.

PAPAGENO:
And now beautiful ladies, if I may, I'd like
to leave.

DREI DAMEN:
Dich empfehlen kannst du immer, doch
bestimmt die Fürstin dich, mit dem Prinzen
ohn' Velweilen nach Sarastros Burg zu
eilen.

THE THREE LADIES:
You can always leave, but the Queen
commands you and the Prince to hurry to
Sarastro's castle without delay.

PAPAGENO:
Nein, dafür bedank' ich mich!
Von euch selbsten hörte ich, daß er wie ein
Tigertier. Sicher ließ' ohn' alle Gnaden
Mich Sarastro rupfen, braten, Setzte mich
den Hunden für.

PAPAGENO:
No thank you!
I myself heard you say that he's like a tiger.
Surely Sarastro would have me
unmercifully plucked and roasted, and I'd
become a tasty meal for his dogs.

DREI DAMEN:
Dich schützt der Prinz, trau' ihm allein.
Dafür sollst du sein Diener sein.

THE THREE LADIES:
Trust the Prince, for he'll protect you, You'll
be his faithful servant.

PAPAGENO:
Daß doch der Prinz beim Teufel wäre!
Mein Leben ist mir lieb;
Am Ende schleicht, bei meiner Ehre,
Er von mir wie ein Dieb.

PAPAGENO: *(to himself)*
Maybe the Prince would risk his life, but I don't want to lose mine. And finally, he may well disappear on me when I need him.

ERSTE DAME:

Hier, nimm dies Kleinod, es ist dein.

FIRST LADY: *(presents Papageno with a box containing chimes: the glockenspiel)*
Here, take this treasure, it's yours.

PAPAGENO:
Ei, ei! Was mag darinnen sein?

PAPAGENO:
Oh, oh, what could be inside?

DREI DAMEN:
Darinnen hörst du Glöckchen tönen.

THE THREE LADIES:
You can hear the bells ringing inside.

PAPAGENO:
Werd' ich sie auch wohl spielen können?

PAPAGENO:
And would I be able to play them too?

DREI DAMEN:
O ganz gewiß! Ja, ja, gewiß!

THE THREE LADIES:
Oh very definitely! Yes, yes, definitely!

ALLE FÜNF:
Silberglöckchen, Zauberflöten
Sind zu eurem/unserm Schutz vonnöten.
Lebet wohl! Wir wollen gehn.
Lebet wohl, auf Wiedersehn!

ALL FIVE:
Silver bells and magic flutes are your/our protection.
Farewell! We're leaving.
Farewell, till we meet again!

TAMINO:
Doch, schöne Damen, saget an...

TAMINO:
But beautiful Ladies, could you please tell us..

PAPAGENO:
Wie man die Burg wohl finden kann?

PAPAGENO:
...where this castle is?

BEIDE:
Wie man die Burg wohl finden kann?

BOTH:
How to find the way to this great castle?

DREI DAMEN:
Drei Knäbchen, jung, schön, hold und weise, Umschweben euch auf eurer Reise.
Sie werden eure Führer sein,
Folgt ihrem Rate ganz allein.

THE THREE LADIES:
Three handsome, kind, and wise young boys will surround you and show you the way. Be sure to follow their advice!

TAMINO, PAPAGENO:
Drei Knäbchen, jung, schön, hold und weise,
Umschweben uns auf unserer Reise.

TAMINO AND PAPAGENO:
Three handsome, kind, and wise young boys will surround us and show us the way.

DREI DAMEN:
Sie werden eure Führer sein,
Folgt ihrem Rate ganz allein.

THREE LADIES:
They will be your guide. Make sure to
follow their advice.

ALLE:
So lebet wohl! Wir wollen gehn.
Lebt wohl, lebt wohl, auf Wiederseh'n!

ALL:
Farewell! We're leaving.
Farewell, farewell, till we meet again!

All depart

ACT I - Scene 2

A room in Sarastro's palace.

SKLAVE:
Ha, ha, ha! Unser Peiniger, der alles
belauschende Mohr, wird morgen sicherlich
gehangen oder gespießt! Pamina entfloh vor
seinen Augen. So ist der Mohr nichts mehr
zu retten, auch wenn Pamina von Sarastros
Gefolge wieder eingefangen würde.

SLAVES:
Ha, ha, ha! Our tyrant, the Moor, will
surely be hung or speared in the morning,
because Pamina escaped from right under
his eyes. Nothing can save the Moor now,
even if Sarastro's men would recapture her.

MONOSTATOS:
He, Sklaven! Schafft Fesseln herbei!

MONOSTATOS:
Hey, Slaves, bring the handcuffs!

SKLAVE:
Fesseln? Doch nicht für Pamina? Der
unbarmherzige Teufel, wie der sie bei den
Händen faßt. Das halt ich nicht aus.

SLAVES:
Handcuffs? We hope they're not for
Pamina? I can't stand it, how the heartless
devil mistreats her.

(Pamina is brought in by the Slaves)

MONOSTATOS:
Du feines Täubchen, nur herein!

MONOSTATOS:
Come in you lovely little dove!

PAMINA:
O welche Marter, welche Pein!

PAMINA:
What torture and pain!

MONOSTATOS:
Verloren ist dein Leben!

MONASTATOS:
Your life is over!

PAMINA:
Der Tod macht mich nicht beben, nur
meine Mutter dauert mich; sie stirbt vor
Gram ganz sicherlich.

MONOSTATOS:
He, Sklaven, legt ihr Fesseln an!
Mein Haß soll dich verderben!

PAMINA:
O laßt mich lieber sterben, Weil nichts,
Barbar, dich rühren kann!

MONOSTATOS:
Nun fort! Laßt mich bei ihr allein!

PAPAGENO:
Wo bin ich wohl? Wo mag ich sein?
Aha! da find' ich Leute, gewagt, ich geh'
hinein.

Schön Mädchen, jung und rein,
viel weißer noch als Kreide.

MONOSTATOS UND PAPAGENO:
Hu! Das ist der Teufel sicherlich!
Hab' Mitleid! Verschone mich!
Hu, hu, hu!

PAMINA:
Mutter - Mutter - Mutter!

Wie? Noch schlägt dieses Herz? Zu neuen
Qualen erwacht?
O das ist hart, sehr hart! Mir bitterer, als der
Tod.

PAMINA:
I'm not afraid to die. I only feel sorry for
my mother, since she will certainly die
from grief.

MONASTATOS:
Hey, Slaves, shackle her!
My hatred will destroy you!

PAMINA:
Tyrant, since you have no compassion, I
prefer to die.

(Pamina becomes unconscious)
MONASTATOS: *(to the Slaves)*
Go away! Leave me alone with her!

PAPAGENO: *(from outside)*
Where am I? Where can I be?
Aha! I see some people, I guess I'll venture
in.

Papageno enters the room and notices Pamina.

Oh what a beauty, so young and pure, and
whiter than snow.

*Monostatos turns around. Papageno is terrified by Monostatos's gaze,
and each becomes frightened by the other.*

MONOSTATOS and PAPAGENO:
Ay! That's the devil for sure!
Have pity! Spare me!
Ay! Ay! Ay!

They both run away, looking back at each other cautiously over their shoulders.

PAMINA: *(dreamlike)*
Mother! Mother! Mother!
(She regains consciousness)

What? This heart is still beating? Did it
awaken to new tortures?
Oh, it's so cruel, so cruel! It's worse than
death!

PAPAGENO
Bin ich nicht ein Narr, daß ich mich
schrecken ließ?
Es gibt doch auch schwarze Vögel auf der Welt,
warum denn nicht auch schwarze Menschen?

Ah, da ist ja das schöne Fräuleinbild noch.
Du Tochter der nächtlichen Königin!

PAMINA:
Nächtlichen Königin? Wer bist du?

PAPAGENO:
Ein Abgesandter der sternflammenden
Königin.

PAMINA:
Meiner Mutter? O Wonne!
Dein Name?

PAPAGENO:
Papageno.

PAMINA:
Papageno? Papageno. Ich erinnere mich,
den Namen oft gehört zu haben, dich selbst
aber sah ich nie.

PAPAGENO:
Ich dich ebensowenig.

PAMINA:
Du kennst also meine gute, zärtliche Mutter?

PAPAGENO:
Wenn du die Tochter der nächtlichen
Königin bist, ja!

PAMINA:
O ich bin es.

PAPAGENO:
Das will ich gleich erkennen.

(Papageno carefully enters)
PAPAGENO:
Am I not a fool to let myself be frightened?
There are black birds in this world, so why
not black people?

(He notices Pamina)
Ah, here's the lovely maiden in the portrait!
The daughter of the Queen of Night!

PAMINA:
Queen of the Night? Who are you?

PAPAGENO:
A messenger from the star-flaming Queen.

PAMINA:
From my mother? How wonderful!
What is your name?

PAPAGENO:
Papageno.

PAMINA:
Papageno? Papageno. I remember having
heard that name often, but I never met you
personally.

PAPAGENO:
I've never met you either.

PAMINA:
So you know my good and loving mother?

PAPAGENO:
If you are the daughter of the Queen of the
Night, yes!

PAMINA:
Yes it's me.

PAPAGENO:
Let me see if it's true.

*Papageno examines the portrait that Tamino received from the Three Ladies,
which he wears on a ribbon around his neck.*

Die Augen schwarz - richtig, schwarz.
Die Lippen rot - richtig rot.
Blonde Haare - blonde Haare.
Alles trifft ein, bis auf Hände und Füße.
Nach dem Gemälde zu schließen,
sollst du weder Hände noch Füße haben;
denn hier sind keine angezegt.

Blue eyes - very blue.
Red lips-very red.
Blond hair-blond hair.
Everything matches, except the hands and
feet. According to the portrait you wouldn't
have hands or feet because they don't show
here.

PAMINA:
Erlaube mir. Ja, ich bin's! Wie kam es in
deine Hände?

PAMINA:
Permit me. Yes, it's me! But how did you
get it?

PAPAGENO:
Ich muß dir das umständlicher erzählen. Ich
kam heute früh, wie gewöhnlich, zu deiner
Mutter Palast mit meiner Lieferung.

PAPAGENO:
I must tell you the details of what happened.
As usual, I went this morning to your
mother's palace to make my delivery.

PAMINA:
Lieferung?

PAMINA:
Delivery?

PAPAGENO:
Ja, ich liefere deiner Mutter schon seit vielen
Jahren alle die schönen Vögel in den Palast.

Ja, und eben, als ich im Begriffe war, meine
Vögel abzugeben, da seh ich einen Menschen
vor mir, der sich Prinz nennen läßt, und dieser
Prinz hat deine Mutter so von sich
eingenommen, daß sie ihm dein Bildnis
schenkte und ihm befahl, dich zu befreien.

Sein Entschluß, der war ebenso rasch, als
seine Liebe zu dir.

PAPAGENO:
Yes, for years I've been delivering all the
beautiful birds to your mother at the palace.

You know, just as I was delivering the
birds, I saw someone who identified
himself as a Prince. The Prince so
impressed your mother, that she gave him
your portrait and ordered him to rescue
you.

He fell in love with you, and immediately
resolved to rescue you.

PAMINA:
Liebe?
Er liebt mich also? O sage mir das noch
einmal, ich höre das Wort Liebe gar zu
gerne.

PAMINA:
Love?
Then he loves me? Please repeat that to me
again, because I love to hear the sound of
that word.

PAPAGENO:
Das glaube ich dir. Bist ja auch ein Fräuleinbild. Kurz also, diese große Liebe zu dir war der Peitschenstreich, um unsre Füße im schnellen Gang zu bringen, und nun sind wir hier, dir tausend schöne und angenehme Sachen zu sagen.

PAMINA:
Freund, wenn Sarastro dich hier erblicken sollte, dann....

PAPAGENO:
So würde mir meine Rückreise erspart blieben - das kann ich mir denken.

PAMINA:
Dein martervoller Tod würde ohne Grenzen sein.

PAPAGENO:
Um diesem auszuweichen, gehn wir lieber beizeiten.

PAMINA:
Wir haben keine Minute zu versäumen.

PAPAGENO:
Ja, komm, du wirst Augen machen, wenn du den schönen Jüngling erblickst.

PAMINA:
Aber wenn dies ein Fallstrick wäre - wenn dieser nun ein böser Geist von Sarastros Gefolge wäre?

PAPAGENO:
Was? Ich ein böser Geist? Wo denkst du hin? Ich bin der beste Geist von der Welt.

PAMINA:
Vergib, vergib, wenn ich dich beleidigte! Du hast ein gefühlvolles Herz.

PAPAGENO:
I believe you because you're a young girl, and therefore the idea of love strikes you like a thunderbolt that urges you to seduce men to cater to you, and shower you with sweet words.

PAMINA:
If Sarastro would see you here, my friend, then....

PAPAGENO:
Then, I have the feeling that I'll never return home.

PAMINA:
You would suffer an agonizing death.

PAPAGENO:
To save our lives, we'd better leave right away.

PAMINA:
We can't waste a minute.

PAPAGENO:
Let's go, you won't believe your eyes when you see this handsome young man.

PAMINA:
But what if this is a trick, and you're a villain employed by Sarastro?

PAPAGENO:
What? Me, a villain? What are you thinking? I'm the most honorable man on earth.

PAMINA:
I'm sorry, forgive me if I have offended you! You're a very sensitive person.

PAPAGENO:
Ja, freilich habe ich ein gefühlvolles
Herz! Aber was nutzt mir denn das alles?
- Ich möcht' mir doch oft alle meine
Federn ausrupfen, wenn ich bedenk', daß
Papageno noch keine Papagena hat.

PAPAGENO:
Yes, I am very sensitive, but what good is
it? I sometimes want to pluck out all my
feathers when I think about the fact that
there still is no Mrs. Papageno.

PAMINA:
Armer Mann! Du hast also noch kein Weib?

PAMINA:
Poor man! So you don't have a wife yet?

PAPAGENO:
Noch nicht einmal ein Mädchen, geschweige
denn ein Weib! Und unsereiner hat eben
auch so seine lustigen Stunden, wo man so
richtig so gesellschaftliche Unterhaltung
haben möcht'.

PAPAGENO:
Not even a girlfriend, let alone a wife. And
every one of us has happy moments which
he would like to share with someone he
loves.

PAMINA:
Geduld, Freund! Der Himmel wird auch
für dich sorgen; er wird dir eine Freundin
schicken, ehe du dir's vermutest.

PAMINA:
Patience, my friend! Heaven will take care
of you too, and send you a girlfriend before
you know it.

PAPAGENO:
Wenn er's nur bald schickte!

PAPAGENO:
If only it would happen soon!

Andantino
PAMINA

Bel Männern, welche Lie - be fühlen, fehlt auch ein gu - tes Her - ze nicht.

PAMINA:
Bei Männern, welche Liebe fühlen, fehlt
auch ein gutes Herze nicht.

PAMINA:
Men who experience love also possess a
good heart.

PAPAGENO:
Die süßen Triebe mitzufühlen, ist dann der
Weiber erste Pflicht.

PAPAGENO:
And it's a wife's priority to share those
sensibilities.

BEIDE:
Wir wollen uns der Liebe freun, wir leben
durch die Lieb' allein.

BOTH:
It's love alone that makes us happy, and
it's love alone that makes life worthwhile.

PAMINA:
Die Lieb' versüßet jede Plage, ihr opfert
jede Kreatur.

PAMINA:
Whatever will happen, it is love that will
heal every sorrow.

PAPAGENO:
Sie würzet unsre Lebenstage, sie wirkt im
Kreise der Natur.

PAPAGENO:
Love perfumes life with its rare fra-
grance, and it's human nature to love.

BEIDE:
Ihr hoher Zweck zeigt deutlich an,
nichts Edler's sei, als Weib und Mann.
Mann und Weib, und Weib und Mann
reichen an die Gottheit an.

BOTH:
For husband and wife, the highest goal in
life is the nobility of love. For husband
and wife, and for wife and husband,
love becomes a divine union.

Pamina and Papageno exit.

ACT I - Scene 3

A sacred grove in which there are three temples:
the Temple of Wisdom, the Temple of Reason, and the Temple of Nature.

The Three Youths appear bearing silver palm branches.
They accompany Tamino whose flute hangs at his side.

DREI KNABEN:
Zum Ziele führt dich diese Bahn, doch
mußt du, Jüngling, männlich siegen. Drum
höre unsre Lehre an: Sei standhaft,
duldsam und verschwiegen!

THE THREE YOUTHS:
This path will lead you to your goal, young
man, but you must be courageous!.
Listen to our advice and be firm, patient,
and discreet.

TAMINO:
Ihr holden Kleinen, sagt mir an, ob ich
Pamina retten kann?

TAMINO:
Tell me boys, do you think that I can rescue
Pamina?

DREI KNABEN:
Dies kundzutun, steht uns nicht an:
Sei standhaft, duldsam und verschwiegen!
Bedenke dies; kurz, sei ein Mann,
Dann, Jüngling, wirst du männlich siegen.

THE THREE YOUTHS:
We don't know, but just be steadfast,
patient and discreet! In short, think of this:
be a man, and you, young man, will
succeed like a man.

The Three Youths depart, leaving Tamino alone.

TAMINO:
Die Weisheitslehre dieser Knaben
Sei ewig mir ins Herz gegraben.
Wo bin ich nun? Was wird mit mir?
Ist dies der Sitz der Götter hier?
Doch zeigen die Pforten, es zeigen die
Säulen, Daß Klugheit und Arbeit und
Künste hier weilen. Wo Tätigkeit thronet
und Müßiggang weicht, erhält seine
Herrschaft das Laster nicht leicht.

Ich wage mich mutig zur Pforte hinein,
die Absicht ist edel und lauter und rein.
Erzitt're, feiger Bösewicht!
Pamina retten ist mir Pflicht.

TAMINO:
I will never forget the wisdom that these
boys taught me.
Where am I now? What will happen to
me? Is this perhaps where the gods
reside?
The portals and columns show that
intelligence and art exist here, and that it
is a place where industry dominates and
vice is nonexistent.

I'll boldly enter through the temple door.
My purpose is noble, good, and pure.
Tremble wretched villain!
To rescue Pamina's is my duty.

He approaches the temple at the right

STIMME:
Zurück!

A VOICE:
Go back!

TAMINO:
Zurück? Zurück? So wag' ich hier mein
Glück!

TAMINO:
Go back? Go back? Then I'll try my luck
over there!

He goes to the temple at the left.

STIMME:
Zurück!

VOICE:
Go back!

TAMINO:
Auch hier ruft man: Zurück!

TAMINO:
Here too they call go back!

He goes to the middle Temple of Wisdom.

Da seh' ich noch eine Tür, Vielleicht find'
ich den Eingang hier.

I see another door over there. Maybe I'll be
able to enter there.

The middle door opens and an old Priest emerges.

ÄLTERER PRIESTER:
Wo willst du, kühner Fremdling, hin?
Was suchst du hier im Heiligtum?

ELDERLY PRIEST:
Where do you want to go, daring stranger?
What are you looking for in this sanctuary?

TAMINO:
Der Lieb' und Tugend Eigentum.

ÄLTERER PRIESTER:
Die Worte sind von hohem Sinn!
Allein wie willst du diese finden?
Dich leitet Lieb' und Tugend nicht,
Weil Tod und Rache dich entzünden.

TAMINO:
Nur Rache für den Bösewicht.

ÄLTERER PRIESTER:
Den wirst du wohl bei uns nicht finden.

TAMINO:
Sarastro herrscht in diesen Gründen?

ÄLTERER PRIESTER:
Ja, ja! Sarastro herrschet hier.

TAMINO:
Doch in dem Weisheitstempel nicht?

ÄLTERER PRIESTER:
Er herrscht im Weisheitstempel hier!

TAMINO:
So ist denn alles Heuchelei!

ÄLTERER PRIESTER:
Willst du schon wieder gehn?

TAMINO:
Ja, ich will gehen, froh und frei, nie euren
Tempel seh'n!

ÄLTERER PRIESTER:
Erklär dich näher mir, dich täuschet ein
Betrug.

TAMINO:
Sarastro wohnet hier, das ist mir schon
genug!

TAMINO:
A place of virtue and of love.

ELDERLY PRIEST:
Your words are certainly noble!
But how do you expect to find these?
You're not guided by love and courage,
but by death and vengeance.

TAMINO:
I'm guided by vengeance on the villain.

ELDERLY PRIEST:
You surely will not find him here.

TAMINO:
Doesn't Sarastro rule here?

ELDERLY PRIEST:
Yes, yes! Sarastro rules here.

TAMINO:
In the Temple of Wisdom?

ELDERLY PRIEST:
Yes, in the Temple of Wisdom!

TAMINO:
So then all of this is hypocrisy!
(Tamino wants to leave)

ELDERLY PRIEST:
You want to leave already?

TAMINO:
Yes, I want to leave, happy and free, and I
never want to see your temple again.

ELDERLY PRIEST:
Explain yourself to me! You are deluded by
deceit.

TAMINO:
The fact that Sarastro lives here is enough
for me.

ÄLTERER PRIESTER:
Wenn du dein Leben liebst, so rede, bleibe
da! Sarastro hassest du?

TAMINO:
Ich haß ihn ewig, ja!

ÄLTERER PRIESTER:
Nun gib mir deine Gründe an.

TAMINO:
Er ist ein Unmensch, ein Tyrann!

ÄLTERER PRIESTER:
Ist das, was du gesagt, erwiesen?

TAMINO:
Durch ein unglücklich Weib bewiesen,
Das Gram und Jammer niederdrückt.

ÄLTERER PRIESTER:
Ein Weib hat also dich berückt?
Ein Weib tut wenig, plaudert viel.
Du, Jüngling, glaubst dem Zungenspiel?

O legte doch Sarastro dir die Absicht seiner
Handlung für!

TAMINO:
Die Absicht ist nur allzu klar!
Riß nicht der Räuber ohn' Erbarmen,
mina aus der Mutter Armen?

ÄLTERER PRIESTER:
Ja, Jüngling, was du sagst, ist wahr.

TAMINO:
Wo ist sie, die er uns geraubt?
Man opferte vielleicht sie schon?

ÄLTERER PRIESTER:
Dir dies zu sagen, teurer Sohn, ist jetztund
mir noch nicht erlaubt.

TAMINO:
Erklär dies Rätsel, täusch' mich nicht!

ELDERLY PRIEST:
If you value your life, speak and stay here!
Do you hate Sarastro?

TAMINO:
I hate him intensely, and I always will!

ELDERLY PRIEST:
Give me your reasons for that!

TAMINO:
He is a brute and a tyrant!

ELDERLY PRIEST:
Do you have proof of what you just said?

TAMINO:
It was proven to me by an unhappy
woman, oppressed by great sorrow.

ELDERLY PRIEST:
So a woman tricked you?
Women do little and talk too much.
You believe this nonsense?

Sarastro has clearly explained the motives
for his action.

TAMINO:
His motive is all too clear!
Didn't the kidnapper tear Pamina unmerci-
fully from her mother's arms?

ELDERLY PRIEST:
Yes, young man, what you say is true.

TAMINO:
Where is the kidnapped victim?
Has she been sacrificed already?

ELDERLY PRIEST:
That my dear boy, I am not allowed to tell
you yet.

TAMINO:
Explain this riddle! Don't deceive me!

ÄLTERER PRIESTER:
Die Zunge bindet Eid und Pflicht.

TAMINO:
Wann also wird die Decke schwinden?

ÄLTERER PRIESTER:
Sobald dich führt der Freundschaft Hand
In's Heiligtum zum ew'gen Band.

ELDERLY PRIEST:
Oath and duty forbid me to talk.

TAMINO:
When will you be able to talk?

ELDERLY PRIEST:
As soon as the hand of friendship leads you
into the sanctuary of the sacred brotherhood.

The Elderly Priest departs.

TAMINO
O ew'ge Nacht! Wann wirst du
schwinden? Wann wird das Licht mein
Auge finden?

STIMMEN:
Bald, Jüngling, oder nie!

TAMINO:
Bald, sagt ihr, oder nie? Ihr Unsichtbaren,
saget mir, lebt denn Pamina noch?

STIMMEN:
Pamina lebet noch!

TAMINO:
Sie lebt! Ich danke euch dafür.

O wenn ich doch imstande wäre,
allmächtige, zu eurer Ehre, mit jedem Tone
meinen Dank zu schildern, wie er hier, entsprang.

TAMINO: *(alone.)*
Oh, eternal night! When will you disappear? When will daylight come?

VOICES: *(from inside the middle temple)*
Soon, young man, or never!

TAMINO:
Soon, you say, or never? Tell me, invisible
ones, is Pamina still alive?

VOICES:
Pamina is still alive!

TAMINO: *(happily)*
She's alive! Thank you so much.

(Tamino takes his flute in his hand.)
Oh, almighty ones, if only I had the
opportunity to honor you and express my
thanks with each tone of my flute.

*Tamino plays the flute, and wild animals and birds of every kind appear to listen.
When he stops playing, they flee.*

Wie stark ist nicht dein Zauberton,
weil, holde Flöte, durch dein Spielen
selbst wilde Tiere Freude fühlen.
Doch Pamina, nur Pamina bleibt davon!

The sweet melodious tones of your magic
flute have the power to even delight wild
animals.
But only Pamina doesn't come!
(Tamino plays the flute again)

Pamina! Pamina! Höre, höre mich!
Umsonst!

Wo? Ach, wo find' ich dich?

Ha, das ist Papagenos Ton!

Pamina! Pamina! Listen to me playing!
It's hopeless!

(Replays)
Where? Oh, where can I find you?

(Papageno's flute is heard)
Aha, that's the sound of Papageno's flute!

Tamino replays his flute, and Papageno answers as before.

Vielleicht sah er Pamina schon,
Vielleicht eilt sie mit ihm zu mir!
Vielleicht führt mich der Ton zu ihr.

Maybe he's seen Pamina already.
Maybe she's coming with him.
Maybe these flute tones will lead me to her.

Tamino leaves. Papageno and Pamina appear. Monostatos pursues them.

PAMINA, PAPAGENO:
Schnelle Füße, rascher Mut
schützt vor Feindes List und Wut.
Fänden wir Tamino doch,
sonst erwischen sie uns noch.

PAMINA AND PAPAGENO:
Quick steps and dauntless courage may
save us from the foe's dreadful rage.
If only we could find Tamino, otherwise
we'll surely be captured!

PAMINA:
Holder Jüngling!

PAMINA: *(calling to Tamino)*
Handsome young man!

PAPAGENO:
Stille, stille, ich kann's besser!

PAPAGENO:
Quiet, I can do it better.

Papageno whistles, and Tamino answers with his flute.

BEIDE:
Welche Freude ist wohl größer?
Freund Tamino hört uns schon.

Hierher kam der Flötenton.
Welch ein Glück, wenn ich ihn finde.
Nur geschwinde! Nur geschwinde!

BOTH:
Could anything make me happier?
Our friend Tamino hears us now.
(pointing in the direction)
There's where the flute sounds came from.
Oh, how wonderful if I would find him!
Let's hurry! Let's hurry!

Monostatos confronts them.

MONOSTATOS:
Nur geschwinde! Nur geschwinde!
Ha, hab' ich euch noch erwischt?

Nur herbei mit Stahl und Eisen.

Wart', ich will euch Mores weisen.
den Monostatos berücken!
Nur herbei mit Band und Stricken,
he, ihr Sklaven, kommt herbei!

MONOSTATOS: *(mocking Pamina)*
Let's hurry! Let's hurry!
Ha, ha, I've caught you?
(calling his Slaves)
Quickly, chain them!
(to Pamina and Papageno)
Wait, I'll show you how to deceive
Monostatos!
Slaves, come over here and chain them!.

PAMINA, PAPAGENO:
Ach, nun ist's mit uns vorbei!

PAMINA , PAPAGENO:
Oh, we're finished!

PAPAGENO:
Wer viel wagt, gewinnt oft viel!
Komm, du schönes Glockenspiel,
laß die Glöckchen klingen, klingen,
daß die Ohren ihnen singen.

PAPAGENO:
One who dares often gains alot!
Come, magic set of bells, let your tones fill
the air and resound in every ear.

(Papageno plays the Glockenspiel)

MONOSTATOS, SKLAVEN:

Das klinget so herrlich,
das klinget so schön!
Larala la la larala la la larala!
Nie hab' ich so etwas gehört und geseh'n!
Larala la la larala la la larala!

MONOSTATOS AND THE SLAVES:
*(Subdued by the sound, Monostatos and
the Slaves sing and dance.)*
It sounds so delightful,
Its sound is so beautiful!
Tralala, lalala, tralalalala!
Oh, I've never heard anything like it!
Tralalala, trala lalala!

(They leave while singing and dancing)

PAMINA, PAPAGENO:
Könnte jeder brave Mann solche
Glöckchen finden!

Seine Feinde würden dann ohne Mühe
schwinden, und er lebte ohne sie
in der besten Harmonie!

Nur der Freundschaft Harmonie mildert die
Beschwerden; ohne diese Sympathie
ist kein Glück auf Erden.

PAPAGENO AND PAMINA:
If only everyone could own such magic
bells!

Then all enemies would easily disappear,
and without them, everyone would live
in great harmony!

Only the harmony of friendship softens
every misfortune. And without this good
feeling, there can be no happiness on earth.

A fanfare of trumpets and drums are heard.

CHOR:
Es lebe Sarastro! Sarastro lebe!

VOICES:
Long live Sarastro! Sarastro lives!

PAPAGENO:
Was soll das bedeuten? Ich zittre, ich bebe!

PAPAGENO:
What's all this about? I'm trembling and shuddering!

PAMINA:
O Freund, nun ist's um uns getan, dies kündigt den Sarastro an!

PAMINA:
Oh my friend, we're finished! It announces that Sarastro is coming!

PAPAGENO:
O wär ich eine Maus, wie wollt' ich mich verstecken!
Wär ich so klein wie Schnecken, so kröch' ich in mein Haus!
Mein Kind, was werden wir nun sprechen?

PAPAGENO:
Oh, if only I were a mouse, then I could hide!
If I were as small as a snail, I'd crawl in my house.
My dear child, what are we going to say?

PAMINA:
Die Wahrheit! Die Wahrheit, sei sie auch Verbrechen.

PAMINA:
The truth! The truth, no matter what!

CHOR:
Es lebe Sarastro! Sarastro soll leben!
Er ist es, dem wir uns mit Freuden ergeben!
Stets mög' er des Lebens als Weiser sich freun, er ist unser Abgott, dem alle sich weihn.

(Sarastro enters with his retinue)
CHORUS:
Long live Sarastro! Sarastro shall live!
We are all devoted to him!
As a wise man, may he enjoy life forever.
He is our idol whom we worship and love!

PAMINA:
Herr, ich bin zwar Verbrecherin,
ich wollte deiner Macht entfliehn,
Allein die Schuld ist nicht an mir,
der böse Mohr verlangte Liebe;
darum, o Herr, entfloh ich dir.
Er ist's!

PAMINA: *(kneels)*
Oh Lord, it's true that I am guilty, because I wished to flee from your power.
But it's not my fault.
I escaped because the wicked Moor desired my love.
He is the guilty one!

SARASTRO:
Steh auf, erheitre dich, o Liebe!
Denn ohne erst in dich zu dringen,
weiß ich von deinem Herzen mehr:
du liebest einen andern sehr.
Zur Liebe will ich dich nicht zwingen,
doch geb' ich dir die Freiheit nicht.

SARASTRO:
Get up, my love, and be happy!
I need not question you further, for I know what is in your heart:
you already love another very much.
Although I will never compel you to love,
I cannot give you your freedom.

PAMINA:
Mich rufet ja die Kindespflicht,
denn meine Mutter...

PAMINA:
A child's duty calls me, because my
mother....

SARASTRO:
...steht in meiner Macht. Du würdest um
dein Glück gebracht, wenn ich dich ihren
Händen ließe.

SARASTRO:
...is in my power. Your happiness would be
ended if I would return you to her.

PAMINA:
Mir klingt der Muttername süße; sie ist es...

PAMINA:
The mention of the word mother sounds so
sweet to me. It is she who is . . . .

SARASTRO:
...und ein stolzes Weib!
Ein Mann muß eure Herzen leiten,
denn ohne ihn pflegt jedes Weib
aus ihrem Wirkungskreis zu schreiten.

SARASTRO:
...a haughty woman!
Only a man should guide women's hearts,
because without man, every woman would
stray.

MONOSTATOS:
Nun stolzer Jüngling, nur hierher!
Hier ist Sarastro, unser Herr.

MONOSTATOS: *(to Tamino)*
Proud young man, come here!
This is Sarastro, our dear lord.

PAMINA:
Er ist's!

PAMINA: *(seeing Tamino for the first time)*
It's him!

TAMINO:
Sie ist's!

TAMINO: *(seeing Pamina)*
It's her!

PAMINA:
Ich glaub' es kaum!

PAMINA:
I can hardly believe it!

TAMINO:
Sie ist's!

TAMINO:
It's her!

PAMINA:
Er ist's!

PAMINA:
It's him!

TAMINO:
Es ist kein Traum!

TAMINO:
It's not a dream!

PAMINA:
Es schling' mein Arm sich um ihn her!

(They approach each other)
PAMINA:
I would embrace him!

TAMINO:
Es schling' mein Arm sich um sie her!

BEIDE:
Und wenn es auch mein Ende wär!

ALLE:
Was soll das heißen?

MONOSTATOS:
Welch eine Dreistigkeit!

TAMINO:
I would embrace her!

BOTH:
Even if it would kill me!

(Pamina and Tamino)
ALL:
What does that mean?

MONOSTATOS:
How audacious!

He steps between Pamina and Tamino, and separates them.

Gleich auseinander! Das geht zu weit!

Dein Sklave liegt zu deinen Füßen,
laß den verwegnen Frevler büßen!

Bedenk, wie frech der Knabe ist:

durch dieses seltnen Vogels List
wollt er Pamina dir entführen,
allein ich wußt' ihn auszuspüren.
Du kennst mich! Meine Wachsamkeit.

SARASTRO:
Verdient, daß man ihr Lorbeer streut!
He, gebt dem Ehrenmann sogleich.-

MONOSTATOS:
Schon deine Gnade macht mich reich.

SARASTRO:
Nur siebenundsiebenzig Sohlenstreich!

MONOSTATOS:
Ach Herr, den Lohn verhofft' ich nicht!

SARASTRO:
Nicht Dank, es ist ja meine Pflicht!

That's enough! This is going too far!

(Monostatos kneels before Sarastro.)
Your slave kneels before you.
Penalize this presumptuous youth!

Think how impudent this boy is.
(Pointing at Papageno.)
Using the tricks of this rare bird, he wanted
to rob you of Pamina.
But I could track him down. You know me
and my vigilance.

SARASTRO:
He deserves the laurel wreath!
Here, give him his reward.

MONOSTATOS:
Your favor alone enriches me.

SARASTRO:
You're to get a whipping of seventy-seven lashes!

MONOSTATOS:
Ah, sir, I don't merit such a reward!

SARASTRO:
Save your thanks, it's only my duty.

ALLE:
Es lebe Sarastro, der göttliche Weise!
Er lohnet und strafet in ähnlichem Kreise.

ALL:
Long live Sarastro, the divine sage!
He justly punishes and rewards

SARASTRO:
Führt diese beiden Fremdlinge in unsern
Prüfungstempel ein; Bedecket ihre Häupter
dann, sie müssen erst gereinigt sein.

SARASTRO:
Lead these two strangers to our temple of
probation, and cover their heads for they
must first be purified.

Monostatos is led away by slaves.

SCHLUßCHOR:
Wenn Tugend und Gerechtigkeit
den großen Pfad mit Ruhm bestreut,
dann ist die Erd' ein Himmelreich,
und Sterbliche den Göttern gleich.

CHORUS:
When virtue and justice are humanity's
ultimate ideals, then earth is indeed heaven,
and mortal men are like gods!

Veils are placed over the heads of Tamino and Papageno.
Sarastro takes Pamina's hand and goes with her through the middle door.
Tamino and Papageno exit with two Priests.

ACT II – Scene 1

A palm grove in which all of the trees are silver with leaves of gold.
Sarastro and Priests enter.

SARASTRO:
Ihr, in dem Weisheitstempel eingeweihten
Diener der großen Götter Osiris und Isis!
Mit reiner Seele erklär' ich euch, daß unsre
heutige Versammlung eine der wichtigsten
unsrer Zeit ist.
Tamino, ein Königssohn, will ins
Heiligtum des größten Lichtes blicken.
Diesen Tugendhaften zu bewachten, ihm
freundschaftlich die Hand zu bieten, sei
heute eine unsrer wichtigsten Pflichten.

SARASTRO:
You, who are ordained in the Temple of
Wisdom, are servants of the great gods:
Osiris and Isis! With a pure heart I advise
you, that our meeting today is the most
important in our history.
Tamino, a king's son, will gaze into the
sublime light of the sanctuary. Our most
important duty today is to protect this
virtuous youth, and to welcome him
warmly.

ERSTER PRIESTER:
Er besitzt Tugend?

FIRST PRIEST:
Is he virtuous?

SARASTRO:
Tugend!

SARASTRO:
Most virtuous!

ZWEITER PRIESTER:
Auch Verschwiegenheit?

SECOND PRIEST:
Can he maintain his silence?

SARASTRO:
Verschwiegenheit!

SARASTRO:
He can!

DRITTER PRIESTER:
Ist wohltätig?

THIRD PRIEST:
Is he benevolent?

SARASTRO:
Wohltätig! Haltet ihr ihn für würdig, so
folgt meinem Beispiele.

SARASTRO:
He is! If you believe he is worthy, then
follow my example.

They blow three times on their horns.

Gerührt über die Einigkeit eurer Herzen, dankt
Sarastro euch im Namen der Menschheit. Mag
immer das Vorurteil seinen Tadel über uns
Eingeweihte auslassen! Jedoch, das böse
Vorurteil soll schwinden; und es wird
schwinden, sobald Tamino selbst die Größe
unserer schweren Kunst besitzen wird.

Sarastro is moved by the unanimity in your
hearts, and thanks you in the name of all
mankind. May Tamino never judge the
deeds of the ordained! Any of his prejudices
will disappear as soon as he becomes part
of our brotherhood.

Pamina haben die Götter dem holden Jüngling bestimmt; dies ist der Grund, warum ich sie der stolzen Mutter entriß. Das Weib dünkt sich groß zu sein; hofft durch Blendwerk und Aberglauben das Volk zu berücken und unsern festen Tempelblau zu zerstören.

Pamina has been designated by the gods for this noble young man. That is why I kidnapped her from her haughty mother. That woman considers herself great, and hopes to beguile the populace through delusion and superstition, and to destroy the firm foundations of our temples.

Allein, das soll sie nicht. Tamino, der holde Jüngling, soll ihn mit uns befestigen und als Eingeweihter der Tugend Lohn, dem Laster aber Strafe sein.

However, she shall not succeed. Tamino himself shall become one of us, and aid us to strengthen the power of virtue and wisdom.

Three blasts on the horns are repeated.

SPRECHER:
Großer Sarastro, wird Tamino auch die harten Prüfungen, die seiner warten, bekämpfen? Verzeih, daß ich so frei bin, dir meinen Zweifel zu eröffnen! Mich bangt es um den Jüngling. Er ist Prinz!

SPEAKER:
Great Sarastro, will Tamino be able to overcome the difficult ordeals that await him? I apologize for being so forthright by expressing my doubts to you! I am worried for this young man. He is a prince!

SARASTRO:
Noch mehr! Er ist Mensch!

SARASTRO:
But more important than that, he is a man!

SPRECHER:
Wenn es nur aber in seiner frühen Jugend leblos erblaßte?

SPEAKER:
But what if he would die so young?

SARASTRO:
Dann ist er Osiris und Isis gegeben und wird der Götter Freuden früher fühlen als wir.

SARASTRO:
Then he will be given to Osiris and Isis and will experience their celestial joys sooner than we.

Three blasts on the horns are repeated.

Man führe Tamino mit seinem eisegefährten in den Vorhof des Tempels ein.

Let Tamino and his companion be led into the court of the temple.

Und du, Freund, vollziehe dein heiliges Amt und lehre sie die Macht der Götter erkennen!

(to the Priest)
And you my friend, fulfill your holy duty and teach them to recognize the might of the gods.

Adagio
SARASTRO

O I - sis und O - si - ris,   schenket der Weisheit Geist dem neu - en Paar!

SARASTRO:
O Isis und Osiris, schenket der Weisheit
Geist dem neuen Paar, die ihr der Wand'rer
Schritte lenket.
Stärkt mit Geduld sie in Gefahr.

CHOR:
Stärkt mit Geduld sie in Gefahr!

SARASTRO:
Laßt sie der Prüfung Früchte sehen;
Doch sollten sie zu Grabe gehen,
So lohnt der Tugend kühnen Lauf,
Nehmt sie in euren Wohnsitz auf.

CHOR:
Nehmt sie in euren Wohnsitz auf.

SARASTRO:
O Isis and Osiris, lead this faithful pair to the
path of wisdom! Concede your blessed
protection, strengthen their hearts and fortify
them with patience when they are in danger.

CHORUS:
Fortify them with patience when they are in
danger.

SARASTRO.
Grant that they bear the trial bravely, and
that their prayers are not denied. But if you
have fated them to fail, please take them,
and grant them life beyond the tomb.

CHORUS:
Grant them life beyond the tomb.

ACT II - Scene 2

The courtyard of the temple. It is night.
Tamino and Papageno are led in by the Speaker and the Second Priests.
Before departing, they remove the veils from Tamino and Papageno.

TAMINO:
Eine schreckliche Nacht! - Papageno, bist
du noch bei mir?

PAPAGENO:
Ja, freilich!

TAMINO:
Wo denkst du, dass wir uns nun befinden?

TAMINO:
What a horrible night! Papageno are you
still with me?

PAPAGENO:
I most certainly am!

TAMINO:
Where do you think we are now?

PAPAGENO:
Wo? Ja, wenn's nicht so finster wär, wollt'
ich dir das schon sagen, aber so...
Oh!

O weh!

TAMINO:
Was ist's?

PAPAGENO:
Mir wird nicht wohl bei der Sache! Ich
glaube, ich bekomme ein kleines Fieber.

TAMINO:
Pfui, Papageno! Sei ein Mann!

PAPAGENO:
Aber ich wollt', ich wär ein Mädchen!

O! o! o! Das ist mein letzter Augenblick!

PAPAGENO:
Where we are? Well if it were not so dark, I
might be able to tell you, but this way ....
Oh!
(Thunder is heard)
Help!

TAMINO:
What is it?

PAPAGENO:
I don't feel comfortable in this situation! I
have a feeling that ice-cold shivers are
running up and down my spine.

TAMINO:
Shame on you Papageno, be a man!

PAPAGENO:
I wish I were a girl!
(Very loud thunder)
Oh! Oh! Oh! My last hour has come!

The Speaker, Priest, and the Second Priest return. All carry torches.

SPRECHER:
Ihr Fremdlinge, was sucht oder fordert ihr
von uns? Was treibt euch an, in unsere
Mauern zu dringen?

TAMINO:
Freundschaft und Liebe.

ÄLTERER PRIESTER:
Bist du bereit, sie mit deinem Leben zu
erkämpfen?

TAMINO:
Ja!

SPRECHER:
Prinz, noch ist's Zeit zu weichen, einen
Schritt weiter, und es ist zu spät.

SPEAKER:
What are you seeking, or asking from us?
What is your reason for invading our
sanctuary?

TAMINO:
Friendship and love.

ELDERLY PRIEST:
And are you prepared to sacrifice your life
for friendship and love?

TAMINO:
I am!

SPEAKER:
Prince, there is still time to turn back. One
step further and it's too late.

TAMINO:
Weisheitslehre sei mein Sieg; Pamina, das
holde Mädchen, mein Lohn!

TAMINO:
Wisdom will be my victory, and the lovely
Pamina my reward!

SPRECHER:
Du unterziehst dich jeder Prüfung dich?

SPEAKER:
Are you willing to undergo each trial?

TAMINO:
Jeder!

TAMINO:
Every one!

SPRECHER:
Reiche deine Hand mir!

SPEAKER:
Give me your hand!
(They clasp hands)

ZWEITER PRIESTER:
Willst auch du dir Weisheitsliebe
erkämpfen?

SECOND PRIEST: *(to Papageno).*
Will you also fight for the love of
wisdom?

PAPAGENO:
Kämpfen ist meine Sache nicht. Ich verlang
ja im Grunde auch gar keine Weisheit. Ich
bin so ein Naturmensch, der sich mit Schlaf,
Speise und Trank zufriedengibt. Und wenn es
einmal sein könnte, daß ich mir ein hübsches
Weibchen fange.

PAPAGENO:
Fighting is not my business, and in
principal, I really don't desire wisdom
either. I am a son of nature, who is content
with sleep, food, and drink. And if possible,
I would like to find a pretty little wife.

ZWEITER PRIESTER:
Die wirst du nie erhalten, wenn du dich
nicht unseren Prüfungen unterziehst.

SECOND PRIEST:
But you will never obtain one, if you do not
submit to our trial.

PAPAGENO:
Und worin bestehen diese Prüfungen?

PAPAGENO:
And what does this trial consist of?

ZWEITER PRIESTER:
Dich allen unseren Gesetzen zu unterwerfen,
selbst den Tod nicht zu scheuen.

SECOND PRIEST:
To surrender to all our laws, and not shrink
from death.

PAPAGENO:
Ich bleibe ledig!

PAPAGENO:
I'll remain single!

ZWEITER PRIESTER:
Aber wenn du dir ein tugenhaftes, schönes
Mädchen erwerben könntest?

SECOND PRIEST:
But what if you could get a virtuous and
beautiful young girl?

PAPAGENO:
Ich bleibe ledig!

PAPAGENO:
I'll remain single!

ZWEITER PRIESTER:
Wenn nun aber Sarastro dir ein Mädchen
aufbewahrt hätte, das an Farbe und
Kleidung dir ganz gleich wäre?

SECOND PRIEST:
But what if Sarastro already has reserved a
virtuous and pretty girl for you, one who is
just like you?

PAPAGENO:
Mir ganz gleich? Ist sie jung?

PAPAGENO:
Just like me? Is she young?

ZWEITER PRIESTER:
Jung und schön!

SECOND PRIEST:
Young and beautiful!

PAPAGENO:
Und heißt?

PAPAGENO:
And what's her name?

ZWEITER PRIESTER:
Papagena.

SECOND PRIEST:
Papagena.

PAPAGENO:
Wie? Papa...

PAPAGENO:
What? Papa...

ZWEITER PRIESTER:
Papagena.

SECOND PRIEST:
Papagena.

PAPAGENO:
Papagena? Haha, die möcht ich aus bloßer
Neugierde schon sehen.

PAPAGENO:
Papagena? Ha ha, and just out of curiosity,
I'd like to see her.

ZWEITER PRIESTER:
Sehen kannst du sie!

SECOND PRIEST:
You can see her!

PAPAGENO:
Aber wenn....Ich bleibe ledig!ich sie
gesehen habe, hernach muß ich sterben?

PAPAGENO:
But after... I remain single! But after I've
seen her, must I die?
(*Second Priest makes a sign of doubt.*)

ZWEITER PRIESTER:
Sehen kannst du sie, aber bis zur verlaufenen
Zeit kein Wort mit ihr sprechen; wird dein
Geist so viel Standhaftigkeit besitzen, deine
Zunge in Schranken zu halten?

SECOND PRIEST:
You can see her, but in the meantime, you
cannot speak to her. Will your mind be
strong enough to control your tongue?

PAPAGENO:
O ja!

PAPAGENO:
Oh, yes!

SPRECHER:
Deine Hand! Du sollst sie sehen.

SPEAKER:
Your hand! You shall see her!
(*They clasp hands*)

ÄLTERER PRIESTER:
Auch dir, Prinz, legen die Götter ein
heilsames Stillschweigen auf; ohne dieses
seid ihr beide verloren. Du wirst Pamina
sehen, aber nie sie sprechen dürfen; dies
ist der Anfang eurer Prüfungszeit.

ELDERLY PRIEST: *(to Tamino)*
The gods impose a holy silence on you
too, my Prince. If you speak, both of you
will be lost. You will see Pamina, but do
not speak to her until the appointed hour.
This the beginning of your trial.

BEIDE PRIESTER:
Bewahret euch vor Weibertücken: dies ist
des Bundes erste Pflicht. Manch weiser
Mann ließ sich berücken, er fehlte und
versah sich's nicht. Verlassen sah er sich
am Ende, vergolten seine Treu' mit Hohn.
Vergebens rang er seine Hände, Tod und
Verzweiflung war sein Lohn.

BOTH PRIESTS:
Your first duty is to be aware of woman's
treachery, because many men found
themselves forsaken, led astray and
ensnared by them. In the end man was all
alone and his faithfulness was met with
scorn. He wrung his hands in vain, for
pain and death were his rewards.

(As it grows dark, both Priests leave)

PAPAGENO:
He, Lichter her! Lichter her! Das ist doch
wunderlich, so oft einen die Herrn
verlassen, sieht man mit offenen Augen
nichts.

PAPAGENO:
Hey! Lights please! It is really amazing. As
soon as these gentlemen leave us, you can't
see anything with your eyes open.

TAMINO:
Ertrag es mit Geduld, und denke, es ist der
Götter Wille.

TAMINO:
Bear it patiently and remember that it is the
will of Gods!

The Three Ladies rush in with torches.

DREI DAMEN:
Wie, wie, wie? Ihr an diesem Schreckensort?
Nie, nie, nie! Kommt ihr wieder glücklich
fort! Tamino, dir ist Tod geschworen! Du,
Papageno, bist verloren!

THE THREE LADIES:
What, what, what? You in this place of
terror? Never, never, never! Get safely out
of here! Tamino, you are destined to die!
Papageno, you are lost!

PAPAGENO:
Nein, nein, das wär' zu viel.

PAPAGENO:
No, no, no, that would be too much!

TAMINO:
Papageno, schweige still! Willst du dein
Gelübde brechen, nicht mit Weibern hier zu
sprechen?

TAMINO:
Papageno, please be quiet!
Do you want to break your oath never to
speak to women?

PAPAGENO:
Du hörst ja, wir sind beide hin.

TAMINO:
Stille, sag ich, schweige still!

PAPAGENO:
Immer still, und immer still!

DREI DAMEN:
Ganz nah' ist euch die Königin!
Sie drang im Tempel heimlich ein.

PAPAGENO:
Wie? Was? Sie soll im Tempel sein?

TAMINO:
Stille, sag' ich, schweige still! Wirst du
immer so vermessen deiner Eidespflicht
vergessen?

DREI DAMEN:
Tamino, hör'! Du bist verloren!
Gedenke an die Königin!
Man zischelt viel sich in die Ohren von
dieser Priester falschem Sinn.

TAMINO:
Ein Weiser prüft und achtet nicht,
Was der gemeine Pöbel spricht.

DREI DAMEN:
Man zischelt viel sich in die Ohren
Von dieser Priester falschem Sinn.
Man sagt, wer ihrem Bunde schwört,
Der fährt zur Höll' mit Haut und Haar.

PAPAGENO:
Das wär', beim Teufel, unerhört!
Sag' an, Tamino, ist das wahr?

TAMINO:
Geschwätz, von Weibern nachgesagt,
Von Heuchlern aber ausgedacht.

PAPAGENO:
Doch sagt es auch die Königin.

PAPAGENO:
You heard it, we're both lost!

TAMINO:
Quiet, I tell you! Please don't talk!

PAPAGENO:
All you say is quiet and don't talk!

THE THREE LADIES:
The Queen is very close by, since she has
secretly entered the temple.

PAPAGENO:
How? What? She's in the temple?

TAMINO:
Quiet, I tell you, don't talk! Will you ever
be so bold to forget the oath you have
sworn?

THE THREE LADIES:
Tamino, listen! You are lost!
Think of the Queen.
Around here, the Priests are whispering
many falsehoods about her.

TAMINO: *(to himself)*
A wise man pays no attention to the talk of
evil people.

THE THREE LADIES:
It's been said that these Priests have
nothing good in mind.
They say that those who join the order are
condemned to hell!

PAPAGENO:
That's outrageous!
Tell me, Tamino, is it true?

TAMINO:
That's nonsense invented by bigots and
repeated by women!

PAPAGENO:
Yet the Queen has said it too.

TAMINO:
Sie ist ein Weib, hat Weibersinn.
Sei still, mein Wort sei dir genug:
Denk' deiner Pflicht und handle klug.

DREI DAMEN:
Warum bist du mit uns so spröde?

Auch Papageno schweigt...so rede!

PAPAGENO:
Ich möchte gerne, woll...

TAMINO:
Still!

PAPAGENO:
Ihr seht, daß ich nicht kann das Plaudern
lassen, ist wahrlich eine Schand' für mich!

TAMINO:
Daß du nicht kannst das Plaudern lassen,
ist wahrlich eine Schand' für dich!

DREI DAMEN:
Wir/Sie müßen sie/uns mit Scham
verlassen, es plaudert keiner sicherlich.

TAMINO, PAPAGENO:
Von festem Geiste ist ein Mann,
er denket, was er sprechen kann.

TAMINO:
She's just like all women.
Take my word for it and hold your tongue.
Think of your duty and be smart!

THE THREE LADIES: *(to Tamino)*
Why are you so cold and callous?

*(Tamino intimates to them that he is not
allowed to speak.)*
And Papageno also doesn't talk! Speak!

PAPAGENO: *(aside to the Ladies).*
I would li.......

TAMINO:
Be quiet!

PAPAGENO: *(aside to the Ladies)*
You see that the fact I can't stop talking is
really a disgrace!

TAMINO:
The fact that you can't stop talking is really
a disgrace!

THREE LADIES:
We're humiliated and better leave them
now because no one is talking to us.

TAMINO, PAPAGENO:
The man who thinks before he speaks
certainly has sound judgment.

As the Three Ladies are about to go, the Priests are heard from inside the Temple.

PRIESTERS:
Entweiht ist die heilige Schwelle!
Hinab mit den Weibern zur Hölle!

CHORUS OF PRIESTS:
The sacred threshold is defiled!
Condemn the women to death and damnation!

(Thunder and lightning)

DREI DAMEN:
O weh! O weh! O weh!

THE THREE LADIES: *(rushing away)*
Oh what misery and grief!

PAPAGENO:
O weh, o weh, o weh!

PAPAGENO: *(falls down in fright)*
Oh what misery and grief!

The Priests enter carrying torches.

SPRECHER:
Heil dir, Jüngling! Dein standhaft
männliches Betragen hat gesiegt. Wir
wollen also mit reinem Herzen unsere
Wanderschaft weiter fortsetzen.

So! Nun komm!

SPEAKER:
Hail young man! Your steadfast, manly
behavior has won a victory! Therefore,
because of your virtue, we wish to continue
our travels.
(The Priest veils Tamino)
Come then!

The Priest and Tamino leave.

ZWEITER PRIESTER:
Was seh ich, Freund! Stehe auf! Wie ist dir?

SECOND PRIEST:
What do I see my friend? Get up! What has
happened to you?

PAPAGENO:
Ich lieg' in einer Ohnmacht!

PAPAGENO:
I'm lying here helpless!

ZWEITER PRIESTER:
Auf! Sammle dich, und sei ein Mann!

SECOND PRIEST:
Get up! Get yourself together and be a man!

PAPAGENO:
Aber sagt mir nur, meine lieben Herren,
warum muß ich denn alle diese Qualen und
Schrecken empfinden? Wenn mir ja die
Götter eine Papagena bestimmten, warum
denn mit so viel Gefahren sie erringen?

PAPAGENO:
But tell me, my dear gentlemen, why do I
have to be subjected to all these torments
and horrors? If the gods really have
destined a Papagena for me, why do I have
to endanger myself to win her?

ZWEITER PRIESTER:
Diese neugierige Frage mag deine vernunft
dir beantworten. Komm! Meine Pflicht ist
allein, dich weiterzuführen.

SECOND PRIEST:
Let your own reason answer your own
inquisitive question. Come, my only duty is
to lead you forward..

The Priest covers Papageno's head with a veil.

PAPAGENO:
Bei so einer ewigen Wanderschaft, da
möcht' einem wohl die Liebe auf immer
vergehen.

PAPAGENO:
If I have to wander like this, I'd prefer to
give up love forever.

Papageno leaves with the Second Priest.

ACT II – SCENE 3

A Garden. Pamina sleeps, the moon shining on her face. Monostatos arrives.

MONOSTATOS:
Ha, da find' ich ja die spröde Schöne!
Welcher Mensch würde bei so einem
Anblick kalt und unempfindlich bleiben?

Das Feuer, das in mir glimmt, wird mich
noch verzehren! Wenn ich wüßte - daß ich
so ganz allein und unbelauscht wäre - ich
wagte es noch einmal.

Das Mädchen wird noch um meinen
Verstand mich bringen.es ist doch eine
verdammte närrische Sache um die Liebe!
Ein Küßchen, dächte ich, ließe sich
entschuldigen.

MONOSTATOS:
Ah, here is the delicate beauty. What
human being could remain cold and
insensitive to such a vision?

The fire that burns within me will consume
me yet! If I only knew that I was alone and
that no one was looking, I'd dare one more
time.

This girl will make me lose my mind yet.
Love is such a crazy thing. I would think a
little kiss would be excusable.

Allegro
MONOSTATOS

Al - les fühlt der Lie-be   Freuden, schnäbelt, tändelt, herzt und küsst.

Alles fühlt der Liebe Freuden, schnäbelt,
tändelt, herzt und küßt; Und ich sollt' die Liebe
meiden, Weil ein Schwarzer häßlich ist!

Ist mir denn kein Herz gegeben? Bin ich
nicht von Fleisch und Blut? Immer ohne
Weibchen leben, Wäre wahrlich Höllenglut!

Drum so will ich, weil ich lebe,
Schnäbeln, küssen, zärtlich sein!
Lieber guter Mond, vergebe,
Eine Weiße nahm mich ein.
Weiß ist schön! Ich muß sie küssen;
Mond, verstecke dich dazu!
Sollt' es dich zu sehr verdrießen,
O so mach' die Augen zu!

Everybody enjoys love with its caresses and
embraces, and I'm supposed to
relinquish love because my skin is dark.

Don't I have a heart within me? Am I not
made of flesh and blood? It is pure hell to
have to live without a woman.

That's why, while I'm still alive, I want
kisses and tenderness.
Dear good moon, please forgive me,
because a white maiden has enticed me.
Her white skin is beautiful, and I must kiss
her. Moon, hide yourself for a moment, and
if it disturbs your bliss, then close your
eyes!

As Monostatos creeps toward Pamina,
the Queen suddenly appears amid thunder and lightning.

KÖNIGIN:
Zurück!

QUEEN: *(to Monostatos)*
Go back!

PAMINA:
Ihr Götter!

PAMINA: *(Pamina awakens)*
Oh Gods!

MONOSTATOS:
O weh! Das ist...die Göttin der Nacht!

MONOSTATOS: *(backing away)*
What's this...the Queen of the Night!

PAMINA:
Mutter! Mutter! Meine Mutter!

PAMINA: *(arising)*
Mother, mother, my mother!
(She falls into her mother's arms.)

MONOSTATOS:
Mutter? Hm, das muß man von weitem
belauschen.

MONOSTATOS:
Mother? Hm, I ought to spy on them from
a distance.
(Monostatos leaves)

KÖNIGIN:
Wo ist der Jüngling, den ich an dich sandte?

QUEEN:
Where is the young man I had sent to you?

PAMINA:
Er hat sich den Eingeweihten gewidmet.

PAMINA:
He has devoted himself to the order.

KÖNIGIN:
Unglückliche Tochter, nun bist du auf ewig
mir entrissen.

QUEEN:
Oh my unfortunate daughter. Now you will
be forever stolen from me.

PAMINA:
Entrissen? O fliehen wir, liebe Mutter!
Unter deinem Schutz trotz' ich jeder
Gefahr.

PAMINA:
Stolen? Oh let's escape, dear mother!
With your protection, I'll venture every
danger.

KÖNIGIN:
Schutz? Liebes Kind, deine Mutter kann
dich nicht mehr schützen. Mit deines Vaters
Tod ging meine Macht zu Grabe. Übergab
freiwillig den siebenfachen Sonnenkreis den
Eingeweihten; diesen mächtigen
Sonnenkreis trägt Sarastro auf seiner Brust.

QUEEN:
Protection? My dear child, your mother can
no longer protect you. With your father's
death, my power disappeared because I
willfully surrendered the seven-sided sun
shield, the powerful zodiax which
Sarastro know wears on his chest.

The Queen draws out a dagger.

Siehst du hier diesen Stahl? Er ist für
Sarastro geschliffen. Du wirst ihn töten und
den mächtigen Sonnenkreis mir überliefern.

Do you see this dagger? It has been
sharpened for Sarastro. You will kill him,
seize the powerful zodiac, and bring it back
to me.

(She forces Pamina to take the dagger)

PAMINA:
Aber, liebste Mutter!....

PAMINA:
But, dearest mother!....

KÖNIGIN:
Kein Wort!

QUEEN:
Not a word!

Allegro assai
QUEEN OF THE NIGHT

Der Höl - le Ra - che kocht in meinem Herzen, Tod und Verzweiflung,

Der Hölle Rache kocht in meinem Herzen,
Tod und Verzweiflung, flammet um mich her!

Hell's revenge is raging in my heart.
Death and despair wildly flame around!

Fühlt nicht durch dich Sarastro
Todesschmerzen, so bist du meine Tochter
nimmermehr. Verstoßen sei auf ewig,
verlassen sei auf ewig.

Go forth, and bear my vengeance to
Sarastro, or as my daughter, you shall be
disowned, and be forever rejected and
forsaken.

Zertrümmert sei'n auf ewig alle Bande der
Natur, Wenn nicht durch dich Sarastro wird
erblassen!
Hört, Rachegötter, hört der Mutter Schwur!

Our natural bond will be destroyed forever
if you do not kill Sarastro!
Hear, gods of vengeance, hear a mother's
curse!

(The Queen disappears amidst thunder)

PAMINA:
Morden soll ich? Götter, das kann ich
nicht! Götter, was soll ich tun?

PAMINA: *(with dagger in hand).*
I must kill someone? Gods, I can't do that!
Gods, what shall I do?

MONOSTATOS:
Dich mir anvertrauen.

MONOSTATOS: *(taking her dagger).*
Trust me.

PAMINA:
Ha!

PAMINA: *(frightened).*
Ha!

MONOSTATOS:
Warum zitterst du? Vor meiner schwarzen
Farbe, oder vor dem ausgedachten Mord?

MONOSTATOS:
Why do you tremble? Is it because of my black
skin or because you have murderous intensions?

PAMINA:
Du weißt also?

PAMINA: *(timidly).*
Then you know?

MONOSTATOS:
Alles. Du hast also nur einen Weg, dich
und deine Mutter zu retten.

MONOSTATOS:
I know everything. There is only one way
to save yourself and your mother.

PAMINA:
Der wäre?

PAMINA:
Which is?

MONOSTATOS:
Mich zu lieben! Ja oder nein?

MONOSTATOS:
To love me! Yes or no?

PAMINA:
Nein!

PAMINA: *(trembling)*
No!

MONOSTATOS:
Nein? Liebe oder Tod!

MONOSTATOS: *(angrily)*
No? Love or death!

PAMINA:
Nien!

PAMINA: *(decidedly)*
No!

MONOSTATOS:
Nein?

MONOSTATOS:
No?

Sarastro comes between them, raises a threatening arm, and hurls Monostatos back.

MONOSTATOS:

So fahre denn hin! Herr, man hat deinen Tod
geschworen, darum wollt' ich dich rächen.

MONOSTATOS:
*(raises the dagger, and then falls before
Sarastro)*
I am not guilty! Sir, since they swore to kill
you, I sought revenge for you.

SARASTRO:
Ich weiß nur allzuviel. Ich weiß, daß deine Seele
ebenso schwarz als dein Gesicht ist. Geh!

SARASTRO:
I know enough. I know that your soul is as
dark as your face. Go!

MONOSTATOS:
Jetzt such' ich die Mutter auf, weil mir die
Tochter nicht beschieden ist.

MONOSTATOS: *(as he leaves)*
Since the daughter is not meant for me,
I'll conspire with the mother.
(Monostatos leaves)

PAMINA:
Herr, strafe meine Mutter nicht! Der
Schmerz über meine Abwesenheit...

PAMINA:
Sir, do not punish my mother! Her sorrow
due to my absence...

SARASTRO::

Ich weiß alles. Weiß, daß sie in
unterirdischen Gemächern des Tempels
herumirrt und Rache über mich und die
Menschheit kocht; allein, du sollst sehen,
wie ich mich an deiner Mutter räche.

SARASTRO:

I know everything. I know that she is
roaming between the walls of the temple,
seeking revenge on me and mankind. But, I
will show you how I take vengeance upon
your mother.

Larghetto
SARASTRO

In die - sen heil - gen Hallen kennt man die Ra - che nicht,

In diesen heilgen Hallen Kennt man die
Rache nicht, und ist ein Mensch gefallen,
Führt Liebe ihn zur Pflicht. Dann wandelt
er an Freundes Hand vergnügt und froh
in's bess're Land.

Within these sacred walls, revenge and
sorrow do not exist. When a man has
failed, only love will guide him to do his
duty. Then he'll walk happily to a better
life, guided by the hand of friendship.

In diesen heil'gen Mauern, wo Mensch den
Menschen liebt, kann kein Verräter lauern,
weil man dem Feind vergibt.
Wen solche Lehren nicht erfreun, verdienet
nicht ein Mensch zu sein.

Within these sacred walls, where man loves
his fellow man, there is no treachery,
because enemies are forgiven. Whoever
does not appreciate this knowledge, does not
deserve to walk this earth.

Pamina and Sarastro exit.

ACT II - Scene 4

A hall in the Temple of Probation.
Tamino and Papageno, unveiled, are led in by the two Priests.

SPRECHER:
Hier seid ihr euch beide allein überlassen.
Sobald die Posaune tönt, dann nehmt ihr
euren Weg dahin. Prinz, lebt wohl! Noch
einmal, vergeßt das Wort nicht: Schweigen.

SPEAKER:
You are on your own but dependent upon
each other. As soon as you hear the sound
of the trumpet, start on your way.
Farewell, Prince. Once more, don't forget,
you are committed to silence.
(The Priest exits)

ZWEITER PRIESTER:
Papageno, wer an diesem Ort sein
Stillschweigen bricht, den strafen die
Götter durch Donner und Blitz. Leb wohl!

SECOND PRIEST:
Papageno, anyone who breaks his silence
in this palace is punished by the gods with
thunder and lightning. Farewell.
(The Second Priest exits)

PAPAGENO:
Tamino!

PAPAGENO:
Tamino!

TAMINO:
St!

TAMINO:
Ssh!

PAPAGENO:
Das ist ein lustiges Leben! Wär' ich lieber in
meiner Strohhütte, oder im Wald, da hör ich
doch noch manchmal einen Vogel pfeifen.

PAPAGENO:
What a jolly life this is! I'd rather be in my
straw hut or in the woods; at least there I'd
hear a bird singing once in a while.

TAMINO:
St!

TAMINO:
Ssh!

PAPAGENO:
Also, mit mir selber werd ich ja vielleicht
noch reden dürfen; und auch wir zwei, wir
können miteinander sprechen, wir sind ja
Männer. La la la-la la la!

PAPAGENO:
Well, at least I'm allowed to talk to myself!
And of course, the two of us can talk to
each other, because we are men!
La la la-la la la!

TAMINO:
St!

TAMINO: *(reprimanding him)*
Ssh!

PAPAGENO:
Nicht einmal einen Tropfen Wasser
bekommt man bei diesen Leuten; viel
weniger sonst was.

PAPAGENO:
One doesn't even get a single drop of water
from these people, let alone anything else.

An old, ugly woman appears, bearing a large cup of water.
Papageno stares at her for a long time.

Ist das für mich?

Is that for me?

ALTES WEIB:
Ja, mein Engel!

OLD WOMAN:
Yes my angel!

PAPAGENO:
Wasser! Nicht mehr und nicht weniger als
Wasser. Sag du mir, du unbekannte
Schöne, werden alle fremden Gäste auf
diese Art bewirtet?

PAPAGENO: *(he drinks)*
Water! Nothing more or less than water.
Tell me, unknown beauty, are all foreign
guests treated this way?

ALTES WEIB:
Freilich, mein Engel!

OLD WOMAN:
Surely my angel!

PAPAGENO:
So, so! Auf diese Art werden die Fremden
auch nicht gar zu häufig kommen.

PAPAGENO:
Is that so? In that case, I guess the
foreigners don't come too frequently.

ALTES WEIB:
Sehr wenig.

OLD WOMAN:
Very seldom.

PAPAGENO:
Das kann ich mir denken. Geh, komm,
Alte, setze dich ein bisser! Her zu mir, mir
ist die Zeit verdammt lang.
Sag du mir, wie alt bist denn du?

PAPAGENO:
That's what I thought. Come, old woman,
sit down next to me for a while. I feel
terribly bored here. *(She sits down by his side)*
Tell me how old you are?

ALTES WEIB:
Wie alt?

OLD WOMAN:
How old?

PAPAGENO:
Ja!

PAPAGENO:
Yes!

ALTES WEIB:
Achtzehn Jahr und zwei Minuten.

OLD WOMAN:
Eighteen years and two minutes.

PAPAGENO:
Achtzig Jahr?

PAPAGENO:
You're eighty?

ALTES WEIB:
Achtzehn Jahr und zwei Minuten.

OLD WOMAN:
Eighteen years and two minutes.

PAPAGENO::
Achtzehn Jahr und zwei Minuten?

ALTES WEIB:
Ja!

PAPAGENO:
Ha ha ha! Ei, du junger Engel! Sag mal,
hast du auch einen Geliebten?

ALTES WEIB:
Ei, freilich, mein Engel!

PAPAGENO:
Ist er auch so jung wie du?

ALTES WEIB:
Nicht gar, er ist um zehn Jahre älter.

PAPAGENO:
Was, um zehn Jahre ist der noch älter als
du? Das muß ja eine feurige Liebe sein!
Und wie nennt sich denn dein Liebhaber?

ALTES WEIB:
Papageno!

PAPAGENO:
Papageno? Wo ist er denn, dieser
Papageno?

ALTES WEIB:
Da sitzt er, mein Engel!

PAPAGENO:
Was, ich wär dein Geliebter?

ALTES WEIB:
Ja, mein Engel!

PAPAGENO:
Sag du mir, wie heißt du denn?

ALTES WEIB:
Ich heiße....

PAPAGENO:
Eighteen years and two minutes?

OLD WOMAN:
Yes!

PAPAGENO:
Ha ha ha! You're really a very young angel!
Tell me, do you have a sweetheart?

OLD WOMAN:
Of course, my angel!

PAPAGENO:
Is he as young as you are?

OLD WOMAN:
Not quite. He's ten years older.

PAPAGENO:
Ten year older than you are? That must be
quite a passionate love!
What's your sweetheart's name?

OLD WOMAN:
Papageno!

(Papageno falls from his seat)
PAPAGENO:
Papageno? Where is he then, this
Papageno?

OLD WOMAN:
Her is sitting right there!

PAPAGENO:
What! I'm your sweetheart?

OLD WOMAN:
Yes my angel!

PAPAGENO:
Tell me. What is your name?

OLD WOMAN:
My name is....

At the sound of loud thunder, the woman hobbles away.

PAPAGENO:
Oh!

Tamino shakes a warning finger at Papageno.

Nun sprech' ich aber kein Wort mehr!

The Three Youths bring a flute and bells.

DREI KNABEN:
Seid uns zum zweitenmal willkommen,
ihr Männer, in Sarastros Reich,
er schickt, was man euch abgenommen,
die Flöte und die Glöckchen euch.

A golden table covered with food and drink is unveiled.

Wollt ihr die Speisen nicht verschmähen,
so esset, trinket froh davon.
Wenn wir zum drittenmal uns sehen,
ist Freude eures Mutes Lohn.
Tamino, Mut! Nah ist das Ziel.
Du, Papageno, schweige still!

They present the flute to Tamino, the bells to Papageno, and then leave.

PAPAGENO:
Tamino, wollen wir nicht speisen?

Blase du nur fort auf deiner Flöte, ich will
meine Brocken blasen.

Herr Sarastro führt eine gute Küche. Auf
die Art, ja, da will ich schon schweigen,
wenn ich immer solche gute Bissen
bekomme. Nun, ich will sehen, ob auch der
Keller so gut bestellt ist.

Ha! Das ist Götterwein!

PAPAGENO:
Oh!

From now on I won't speak another word!

THE THREE YOUTHS:
For the second time we welcome you to
Sarastro's kingdom. Sarastro is returning
what was taken from you: your flute and
the little bells.

If you like the food on the table,
then drink and eat as much as you want.
When we will see each other for a third
time, it will be to celebrate your courage.
Tamino, courage, your goal is near.
And you Papageno, don't talk!

PAPAGENO:
Tamino, shall we eat?
(Tamino plays his flute)
You just play your flute and I'll play my
own game and eat.

(Papageno goes to the table and eats.)
That Mister Sarastro has a good cook!
With such delicious food, I don't mind
being silent. Now I'll see if his wine cellar
is as good as his kitchen.

(He fills his glass and drinks.)
Ha, this is wine fit for the gods!

As Pamina rushes in, Tamino stops playing his flute.

PAMINA:
Du hier? Gütige Götter! Dank euch! Ich
hörte deine Flöte und so lief ich pfeilschnell
dem Tone nach.
Aber du bist traurig? Sprichst nicht eine
Silbe mit deiner Pamina?

TAMINO:
Ah!

PAMINA:
Ich soll dich meiden? Ich soll dich fliehen,
ohne zu wissen, warum? Tamino, liebst du
mich nicht mehr?
Papageno, sage du mir, sag, was ist
meinem Freund?

PAPAGENO:
Hm, hm, hm.

PAMINA: *(happily).*
You're here? Good gods, I thank you! I
heard the tones of your flute and rushed
toward the sounds.
But you are sad? Don't you even say a
word to your Pamina?

TAMINO:
Ah!
(indicating that she should leave)

PAMINA:
You want me to ignore you? I should leave
you without knowing why? Tamino, don't
you love me anymore?
Papageno, tell me what's the matter with
my friend?

PAPAGENO:
(with full mouth, motions her to leave)
Hm, hm, hm.

Andante

Ach,ich fühl's es ist verschwunden,   e - wig   hin   mein ganzes Glück.

PAMINA:
Ach, ich fühl's es ist verschwunden,
ewig hin der Liebe Glück!
Nimmer kommt ihr Wonnestunden
Meinem Herzen mehr zurück!
Sieh', Tamino, diese Tränen,
Fließen, Trauter, dir allein!
Fühlst du nicht der Liebe Sehnen,
So wird Ruh' im Tode sein!

PAPAGENO:
Nicht wahr, Tamino, ich kann auch
schweigen, wenn's sein muß.
Ja; bei so einem Unternehmen, da bin ich
ein Mann.

Der Koch und der Kellermeister sollen leben!

PAMINA:
Oh, I feel that the happiness of love is gone
forever!
I will never feel joy and happiness again in
my heart.
Look, Tamino, these tears flow just for you!
If you no longer love me, I'd rather die!

(Pamina leaves sadly)

PAPAGENO: *(eats hastily)*
You see, Tamino, I too can keep quiet
when it is necessary.
If I have to, I am a man.

(Papageno drinks)
Long live the cook and the winemaster!

Three trumpet calls are heard, and Tamino indicates that Papageno should leave.

Geh du nur voraus, ich komm dann schon nach.

You go first, and then I'll follow.

(Tamino pushes Papageno to leave)

Nein! Der Stärkere bleibt da!

No! The stronger one stays here!

(The three trumpet calls sound)

Aha, das geht uns an.

Aha, that concerns us.

Wir kommen schon. Aber hör mal, Tamino, was wird denn noch alles mit uns werden?

We're coming. But tell me Tamino, what's going to happen to us?

(Tamino points upwards)

Ach, du meinst, die Götter soll ich fragen?

Do you mean that I should ask the gods?

(Tamino indicates yes)

Ja, die könnten uns freilich mehr sagen, als wir wissen!

Yes, they surely can tell us more than we know!

(The three calls are heard again)

Wile nur nicht so, wir kommen noch immer zeitlich genug, um uns braten zu lassen.

Don't hurry so much. We'll be in time to be roasted.

Tamino drags Papageno away forcefully.

ACT II - Scene 5

Interior vaults of the pyramid.

CHOR DER PRIESTER:
O Isis und Osiris, welche Wonne!
Die düst're Nacht verscheucht der Glanz
der Sonne.
Bald fühlt der edle Jüngling neues Leben:
Bald ist er unserm Dienste ganz ergeben.
Sein Geist ist kühn, sein Herz ist rein,
Bald wird er unser würdig sein.

CHORUS OF THE PRIESTS:
Oh Isis and Osiris, what joy!
The dark night is chased away by the
power of our sun.
Soon the noble youth will feel new life.
Soon he will be in our service and enlightened.
His spirit is brave; his heart is pure.
Soon he will be worthy of us.

(Tamino is brought in)

SARASTRO:
Prinz, dein Betragen war bis hierher männlich
und gelassen; nun hast du noch zwei gefährliche
Wege zu wandern. Schlägt dein Herz noch
ebenso warm für Pamina, und wünschest du
einst als ein weiser Fürst zu regieren, so mögen
die Götter dich ferner begleiten.

Deine Hand! Man bringe Pamina!

SARASTRO:
Prince, until now your behavior has been
manly and composed. But you still have
two obstacles to overcome.
If you heart still beats warmly for Pamina,
and you wish to reign with wisdom in the
future, may the gods guide you.

Give me your hand! Bring Pamina here!

Two Priests go out and return with Pamina, who is veiled.

PAMINA:
Wo bin ich? Welch eine fürchterliche
Stille! Wo ist Tamino?

PAMINA:
Where am I? How terribly quiet it is here?
Where is Tamino?

SARASTRO:
Er wartet deiner, um dir das letzte
Lebewohl zu sagen.

SARASTRO:
He awaits you, to bid you a last farewell.

PAMINA:
Das letzte Lebewohl? O wo ist er?

PAMINA:
A last farewell? Where is he?

SARASTRO:
Hier!

SARASTRO:
Here!

PAMINA:
Tamino!

PAMINA:
Tamino!

TAMINO:
Zurück!

PAMINA:
Soll ich dich, Teurer, nicht mehr seh'n?

SARASTRO:
Ihr werdet froh euch wiedersehn!

PAMINA:
Dein warten tödliche Gefahren!

TAMINO:
Die Götter mögen mich bewahren!

PAMINA:
Dein warten tödliche Gefahren!

TAMINO, SARASTRO:
Die Götter mögen mich/ihn bewahren!

PAMINA:
Du wirst dem Tode nicht entgehen,
Mir flüstert dieses Ahnung ein.

TAMINO, SARASTRO:
Der Götter Wille mag geschehen,
ihr Wink soll mir/ihm Gesetze sein!

PAMINA:
O liebtest du, wie ich dich liebe,
Du würdest nicht so ruhig sein.

TAMINO, SARASTRO:
Glaub mir, ich/er fühle/fühlet gleiche Triebe,
Werd'/Wird ewig dein Getreuer sein.

SARASTRO:
Die Stunde schlägt, nun müßt ihr scheiden!

PAMINA, TAMINO:
Wie bitter sind der Trennung Leiden!

SARASTRO:
Tamino muß nun wieder fort.

TAMINO:
Go back!

PAMINA:
My dear one, will I never see you again?

SARASTRO:
You surely will happily see each other again!

PAMINA:
Deadly dangers await you!

TAMINO:
May the gods protect me!

PAMINA.
Deadly dangers await you!

TAMINO, SARASTRO:
May the gods protect me/him!

PAMINA:
I have the feeling that you will not escape
death.

TAMINO, SARASTRO:
May the will of the gods be done,
and their desire be law for me/him.

PAMINA:
Oh if you loved me as I loved you, then you
surely would not be so calm.

TAMINO, SARASTRO:
Trust me, I/ he loves you with equal
passion, and I/he will love you forever.

SARASTRO:
The hour has come for you to separate!

PAMINA, TAMINO:
How bitter are the pains of separating!

SARASTRO:
Tamino must leave now.

TAMINO:
Pamina, ich muß wirklich fort!

PAMINA:
Tamino muß nun wirklich fort?

SARASTRO:
Nun muß er fort!

TAMINO:
Nun muß ich fort.

PAMINA:
So mußt du fort!

TAMINO:
Pamina, lebe wohl!

PAMINA:
Tamino, lebe wohl!

SARASTRO:
Nun eile fort. Dich ruft dein Wort.
Die Stunde schlägt, wir sehn uns wieder!

TAMINO, PAMINA:
Ach, gold'ne Ruhe, kehre wieder!
Lebe wohl! Lebe wohl!

TAMINO:
Pamina, I really must leave!

PAMINA:
Must Tamino really leave now?

SARASTRO:
Yes, he must leave now!

TAMINO:
Yes, I must leave now!

SARASTRO:
Then you must leave!

TAMINO:
Pamina, farewell!

PAMINA:
Tamino, farewell!

SARASTRO:
Now hurry. Your duty calls you. At the
right time, we'll meet again!

TAMINO, PAMINA:
Oh, may peace return again!
Farewell! Farewell!

Pamina is led away by two Priests. Sarastro leaves with Tamino.

ACT II – Scene 6

A small garden.

PAPAGENO:
Tamino! Tamino! Willst du mich denn gänzlich verlassen?

PAPAGENO: *(from outside)*
Tamino! Tamino! Are you leaving me all alone?

(looking around)

Wenn ich nur wenigstens wüßte, wo ich wäre. Tamino! Tamino, solang ich lebe, geh' ich nicht mehr von dir! Aber dies einmal verlaß mich armen Reisegefährten nicht!

If I only knew where I was! Tamino! Tamino, as long as I live I'll never leave you! Just this once don't desert your poor fellow traveller!

He reaches the door through which Tamino was led away.

EINE STIMME:
Zurück!

VOICE:
Go back!

PAPAGENO:
Barmherzige Götter! Wo wend' ich mich hin! Wenn ich nur wüßte, wo ich hereinkam. Tamino!

PAPAGENO:
Merciful Gods! Where shall I turn? If I only knew where I came in. Tamino!

DIE STIMME:
Zurück!

THE VOICE:
Go back!

(Thunder and flames burst from the door)

PAPAGENO:
Nun kann ich weder vorwärts noch zurück!

Und muß am Ende gar verhungern. Geschieht mir schon recht! Warum bin ich denn auch mitgereist?

PAPAGENO:
Now I can't go either forwards or backwards! *(he cries)*
And I'll have to starve here. Serves me right! Why did I go along with him?

The Speaker, bearing a torch, approaches Papageno.

SPRECHER:
Mensch! Du hättest verdient, auf immer in finsteren Klüften der Erde zu wandern; die gütigen Götter aber entlassen dich der Strafe dich. Dafür aber wirst du das himmlische Vergnügen der Eingeweihten nie fühlen.

SPEAKER:
Man, you deserve to wander forever in the dark recesses of the earth, but the merciful gods exempt you from this punishment. However, you shall never experience the heavenly pleasures of the ordained.

PAPAGENO:
Je nun, es gibt ja noch andere Leute
meinesgleichen! Mir wäre jetzt ein gutes
Glas Wein das größte Vergnügen.

PAPAGENO:
So what, there are many people like me in
the world. At the moment, I'd like nothing
better than a good glass of wine.

ÄLTERER PRIESTER:
Sonst hast du keinen Wunsch in dieser Welt?

ELDERLY PRIEST:
Otherwise, you have no other wish in this world?

PAPAGENO:
Bis jetzt nicht.

PAPAGENO:
So far, no other wish.

SPRECHER:
Man wird dich damit bedienen!

SPEAKER:
It will be coming to you!

After the Priest exits, a large jug filled with wine emerges..

PAPAGENO:
Ach! Da ist er ja schon!

Herrlich! Himmlisch! Göttlich! Ha! Ich bin
jetzt so vergnügt, daß ich bis zur Sonne
fliegen könnte, wenn ich Flügel hätte! Ha!
Mir wird so wunderlich ums Herz! Ich
möchte... ich wünschte... ja, was denn?

PAPAGENO:
Hurray! There it is already!
(He drinks)
Delicious! Heavenly! Divine! Ha! I'm so
delighted now that if I had wings, I could fly
to the sun. Ha! I'm starting to feel so
wonderful! I'd love...I'd wish...... but
what?

Papageno plays the Glockenspiel.

Andante
PAPAGENO

Ein Mädchen o - der   Weib - chen   wünscht   Pa - pa - ge - no   sich,

Ein Mädchen oder Weibchen
wünscht Papageno sich!
O so ein sanftes Täubchen
wär' Seligkeit für mich!

A girl or a little wife is what Papageno
would love to have!
Oh such a gentle turtledove would be pure
heaven!

Dann schmeckte mir Trinken und Essen,
dann könnt' ich mit Fürsten mich messen,
Des Lebens als Weiser mich freun,
und wie im Elysium sein!

Then I'd love to drink and eat,
and measure up to royalty.
I'd enjoy life like a wise man, and feel I had
arrived in Elysium!

Ach, kann ich denn keiner von allen
den reizenden Mädchen gefallen?
Helf' eine mir nur aus der Not,
sonst gräm' ich mich wahrlich zu Tod!
Wird keine mir Liebe gewähren,
So muß mich die Flamme verzehren!
Doch küßt mich ein weiblicher Mund,
So bin ich schon wieder gesund!

Oh, doesn't any fair maiden want me?
Someone please liberate me from my
misery, or else I'll cry myself to death!
If no young girl gives her love to me,
I'll be consumed by flames!
However, if I should receive a woman's
kiss,
I'd be in heavenly bliss!

The old woman, leaning on her cane, happily arrives.

ALTES WEIB:
Da bin ich schon, mein Engel!

OLD WOMAN:
Here I am, my angel!

PAPAGENO:
Was, du hast dich meiner erbarmt?

PAPAGENO:
What, you feel sorry for me?

ALTES WEIB:
Ja, mein Engel!

OLD WOMAN:
Yes, my angel!

PAPAGENO:
Na, das ist ein Glück!

PAPAGENO:
Am I lucky!

ALTES WEIB:
Und wenn du mir versprichst, mir ewig
treu zu bleiben, dann sollst du sehen, wie
zärtlich dein Weibchen dich lieben wird.

OLD WOMAN:
And if you promise to be true to me
forever, then you'll see how tenderly your
little wife will love you.

PAPAGENO:
Ei, du zärtliches Närrchen!

PAPAGENO:
Oh you tender little fool!

ALTES WEIB:
O. wie will ich dich umarmen, dich
liebkosen, dich an mein Herz drücken!

OLD WOMAN:
Oh, how I'll embrace you, caress you, and
press you to my heart!

PAPAGENO:
Auch ans Herz drücken?

PAPAGENO:
Even press me to your heart?

ALTES WEIB::
Komm, reich mir zum Pfand unsers
Bundes deine Hand!

OLD WOMAN:
Come, give me your hand as a pledge of
our union!

PAPAGENO::
Nur nicht so hastig, mein lieber Engel! So ein
Bündnis braucht doch auch seine Überlegung.

PAPAGENO:
Not so fast, my dear angel! After all, such a
union needs some consideration.

ALTES WEIB:
Papageno, ich rate dir, zaudre nicht! -
Deine Hand, oder du bist auf immer hier
eingekerkert.

OLD WOMAN:
Papageno, I advise you not to hesitate. Give
me your hand or you will be imprisoned
here forever.

PAPAGENO:
Eingekerkert?

PAPAGENO:
Imprisoned?

ALTES WEIB:
Wasser und Brot wird deine tägliche Kost
sein. Ohne Freund, ohne Freundin mußt du
leben, und der Welt auf immer entsagen.

OLD WOMAN:
Bread and water will be your daily diet. You
must live without friends or sweetheart, and
renounce the world forever.

PAPAGENO:
Wasser trinken? Der Welt entsagen? Nein,
da will ich doch lieber eine Alte nehmen,
als gar keine. Also gut, da hast du meine
Hand mit der Versicherung, daß ich dir
immer getreu bleibe.
...olang ich keine Schönere sehe.

PAPAGENO:
I have to drink water and renounce the
world? No, then I prefer to have an old
woman than none at all. All right. Here is
my hand with my promise to be true to you
forever.*(aside)*
...as long as I don't see a prettier one.

ALTES WEIB:
Das schwörst du?

OLD WOMAN:
Do you swear to that?

PAPAGENO:
Ja, das schwör' ich!

PAPAGENO:
Yes, I swear to it!

The Old Woman transforms into a young woman, dressed like Papageno.

Papagena!   Papagena!

As he attempts to embrace her, the Priest comes and takes her by the hand.

SPRECHER:
Fort mit dir, junges Weib! Er ist deiner noch
nicht würdig!
Zurück sage ich.

SPEAKER:
Away with you, young woman! He is not
yet worthy of you! *(to Papageno)*
I'm telling you to go back!

PAPAGENO:
Soll ich zurückziehe, soll die Erde mich
verschlingen. O ihr Götter!

PAPAGENO:
Before I go back, the earth will swallow me
up. Oh you gods!

As the Speaker takes Papagena away, Papageno sinks into the earth.

The Three Youths arrive.

Andante
THREE YOUTHS

Bald prangt, den Morgen zu verkünden, die Sonn auf gold - ner Bahn.

DREI KNABEN:
Bald prangt, den Morgen zu verkünden,
die Sonn auf goldner Bahn.
Bald soll der Aberglaube schwinden.
Bald siegt der weise Mann.
O holde Ruhe, steig' hernieder,
kehr' in der Menschen Herzen wieder;
dann ist die Erd' ein Himmelreich,
ind Sterbliche den Göttern gleich.

THE THREE YOUTHS:
Soon the sun will rise to banish the night,
and beam its brilliance on the earth.
Soon all superstition will vanish.
Soon the wise man will be victorious.
Oh heavenly quiet, now descend,
and return to the heart of man.
Then the earth will be as heaven,
and mortals divine.

ERSTER KNABE:
Doch seht, Verzweiflung quält Paminen!

FIRST YOUTH:
But look, Pamina is suffering from doubt!

ZWEITER, DRITTER KNABE:
Wo ist sie denn?

SECOND AND THIRD YOUTH:
Where is she?

ERSTER KNABE:
Sie ist von Sinnen!

FIRST YOUTH:
She is out of her mind!

DREI KNABEN:
Sie quält verschmähter Liebe Leiden.Laßt
uns der Armen Trost bereiten!
Fürwahr, ihr Schicksal geht uns nah!
O wäre nur ihr Jüngling da!
Sie kommt, laßt uns beiseite gehn,
Damit wir, was sie mache, sehn.

THE THREE YOUTHS:
She suffers pangs of scorned love. Let our
embrace console her! Her fate has greatly
moved us! Oh if only her young man
would be here! Oh here she comes.
Let's move aside so we can observe her
better and prevent a fatal mistake.

The Three Youths step aside. Pamina rushes in half insane,
holding the dagger given her by the Queen.

PAMINA:
Du also bist mein Bräutigam?
Durch dich vollend' ich meinen Gram.

PAMINA: *(addressing her dagger)*
So you are my bridegroom?
Through you my grief will be ended!

DREI KNABEN:
Welch dunkle Worte sprach sie da?
Die Arme ist dem Wahnsinn nah.

PAMINA:
Geduld, mein Trauter, ich bin dein;
bald werden wir vermählet sein.

DREI KNABEN:
Wahnsinn tobt ihr im Gehirne;
selbstmord steht auf ihrer Stirne.

Holdes Mädchen, sieh uns an!

PAMINA:
Sterben will ich, weil der Mann,
Den ich nimmermehr kann hassen,
Sein Traute kann verlassen.

Dies gab meine Mutter mir.

DREI KNABEN:
Selbstmord strafet Gott an dir!

PAMINA:
Lieber durch dies Eisen sterben,
als durch Liebesgram verderben!
Mutter, durch dich leide ich,
und dein Fluch verfolget mich!

DREI KNABEN:
Mädchen, willst du mit uns gehn?

PAMINA:
Ha, des Jammers Maß ist voll!
Falscher Jüngling, lebe wohl!
Sieh, Pamina, ach! Stirbt durch dich,
dieses Eisen töte mich!

DREI KNABEN:

Ha, Unglückliche, halt ein! Sollte dies dein
Jüngling sehen, Würde er vor Gram
vergehen; Denn er liebet dich allein.

THE YOUTHS: *(aside)*
Oh, what sinister words did she say?
The poor soul is near madness!

PAMINA:
Patience, my beloved, I am yours. Soon we
will be united.

THE YOUTHS: *(draw nearer)*
Madness lurks in her mind.
She's contemplating suicide.
(To Pamina)
Lovely maiden, listen to us!

PAMINA:
Since I cannot hate the man I love,
and he has forsaken me,
I want to die.
(pointing to the dagger)
This, my mother gave to me.

THE THREE YOUTHS:
God will punish you if you commit suicide!

PAMINA:
I prefer to die by this dagger than to perish
as a grieving lover!
Mother, I suffer because of you, and your
curse that pursues me!

THE THREE YOUTHS:
Girl, do you want to come with us?

PAMINA:
Ah, my suffering is too much!
Faithless lover, farewell!
Look, Pamina dies because of you.
May this dagger kill me!

(She tries to stab herself)

THE THREE YOUTHS:
(snatching the dagger from her)
Stop, unhappy one! If your lover would see
this, he would die from sorrow, for you are
his only love.

PAMINA:
Was? Er fühlte Gegenliebe, und verbarg
mir seine Triebe, Wandte sein Gesicht vor
mir? Warum sprach er nicht mit mir?

DREI KNABEN::
Dieses müßen wir verschweigen, doch wir
wollen dir ihn zeigen! Und du wirst mit
Staunen sehn, daß er dir sein Herz geweiht,
und den Tod für dich nicht scheut. Komm,
wir wollen zu ihm gehen.

PAMINA:
Führt mich hin, ich möcht' ihn seh'n!

ALLE:
Zwei Herzen, die von Liebe brennen,
Kann Menschenohnmacht niemals trennen.
Verloren ist der Feinde Müh',
Die Götter selbst schützen sie.

PAMINA: *(recovering herself)*
What? He loves me, and concealed his
feelings for me and turned his face away?
Why didn't he speak to me?

THE THREE YOUTHS:
This, we're not allowed to tell you, but we
will show him to you! You will be amazed
at how much he loves you, and that he
would sacrifice his life for you. Come, let's
go to him!

PAMINA:
Take me to him, I'd love to see him!

ALL:
Two hearts that are burning with such true
love, humans can never separate.
The efforts of the enemy are in vain, for the
gods are protecting them from harm.

(All leave)

ACT II - Scene 7

Rugged cliffs in the mountains at twilight.
There is a roaring stream, and a brightly glowing fire.

DIE ZWEI GEHARNISCHTEN::
Der, welcher wandert diese Straße voll
Beschwerden, wird rein durch Feuer,
Wasser, Luft und Erden; wenn er des
Todes Schrecken überwinden kann, schwingt
er sich aus der Erde himmelan.Erleuchtet
wird er dann im Stande sein, sich den
Mysterien der Isis ganz zu weih'n.

TWO MEN IN ARMOR:
He who pursues this path full of dangers,
becomes purified by fire, water, air and
earth.
If he can overcome the fear of death, he
will rise to heaven. Thus purified, he then
will be able to devote himself completely to
Isis's mysteries.

TAMINO:
Mich schreckt kein Tod, als Mann zu
handeln, den Weg der Tugend
fortzuwandeln. Schließt mir die
Schreckenspforten auf, ich wage froh den
kühnen Lauf.

TAMINO:
I'm not afraid of death. Even death will not
prevent me from acting as a man, and
from walking the path of virtue. Open up
the dreadful gates, and I'll gladly risk the
dangers!

PAMINA:
Tamino, halt! Ich muß dich sehn.

PAMINA: *(from within)*
Tamino, stop! I must see you!

TAMINO:
Was hör ich? Paminens Stimme?

TAMINO:
What do I hear? Pamina's voice?

DIE GEHARNISCHTEN::
Ja, ja, das ist Paminens Stimme.

MEN:
Yes, yes, that is Pamina's voice.

ALLE:
Wohl mir/dir, nun kann sie mit mir/dir
geh'n, nun trennet uns/euch kein Schicksal
mehr, wenn auch der Tod beschieden wär!

ALL:
Fortunate me/you, now she can come with
me/you. Destiny will no longer separate us/
you, even in death!

TAMINO:
Ist mir erlaubt, mit ihr zu sprechen?

TAMINO:
Am I allowed to speak to her?

DIE GEHARNISCHTEN::
Dir ist erlaubt, mit ihr zu sprechen.

MEN:
You are allowed to speak to her.

ALLE:
Welch Glück, wenn wir uns/euch
wiederseh'n. Froh Hand in Hand in Tempel
geh'n! Ein Weib, das Nacht und Tod nicht
scheut, ist würdig und wird eingeweiht.

ALL:
What joy when we will see you/each other
again. Enter the temple joyfully, hand in
hand. A wife unafraid of night and death,
deserves to be ordained.

Priests bring in Pamina, and Pamina and Tamino embrace.

PAMINA:
Tamino mein! O welch ein Glück!

PAMINA:
My dear Tamino! What happiness this is!

TAMINO: ·
Pamina mein! O welch ein Glück!

TAMINO:
My dear Pamina! What happiness this is!
(He points to both mountain caverns)
Here are the gates of horror that threaten
me with danger and death.

Hier sind die Schreckenspforten,
Die Not und Tod mir dräu'n.

PAMINA:
Ich werde aller Orten an deiner Seite sein;
Ich selbsten führe dich, die Liebe leitet mich!

Sie mag den Weg mit Rosen streun, weil
Rosen stets bei Dornen sein. Spiel du die
Zauberflöte an; Sie schütze uns auf uns'rer
Bahn.
Es schnitt in einer Zauberstunde. Mein Vater
sie aus tiefstem Grunde Der tausendjähr'gen
Eiche aus, Bei Blitz und Donner, Sturm und
Braus. Nun komm und spiel' die Flöte an, Sie
leite uns auf grauser Bahn.

PAMINA:
I will always be by your side. I myself will
lead you, for I am guided by love.

(Pamina takes Tamino by the hand)
Although our path will be strewn with
thorny roses, our love will prevail. Now
you'll play your magic flute. It will protect
us on our way.
My father used his magical powers to
fashion it himself from a thousand-year old
oak tree during thunder, lightning, storm
and gale. Now play your magic flute, for it
will protect us on our way.

TAMINO, PAMINA:
Wir wandeln (Ihr wandelt) durch des Tones
Macht Froh durch des Todes düstre Nacht.

TAMINO, PAMINA:
With the flute's power, we wander (you
wander) happily through death's darkness.

Tamino and Pamina pass through the fiery cave while he plays the flute.
As soon as they emerge from the ordeal of fire, they embrace.

PAMINA, TAMINO:
Wir wandelten durch Feuersgluten,
Bekämpften mutig die Gefahr.

Dein Ton sei Schutz in Wasserfluten,
So wie er es im Feuer war.

PAMINA, TAMINO:
We wandered through the flames, and
bravely overcame the dangers.
(to the flute)
May your tones protect us in the flood of
waters, as they did in the fires.

Tamino and Pamina proceed into the cave of water,
and emerge shortly thereafter.

PAMINA, TAMINO:
Ihr Götter, welch ein Augenblick!
Gewähret ist uns Isis' Glück!

PAMINA, TAMINO:
Oh gods, what a glorious sight!
The joy of Isis is upon us!

CHOR: :
Triumph! Triumph! Du edles Paar!
Besieget hast du die Gefahr!
Der Isis Weihe ist nun dein!
Kommt, tretet in den Tempel ein!

CHORUS OF PRIESTS:
Triumph! Triumph! You noble pair!
You have overcome the danger!
You are now consecrated to Isis!
Come, enter the temple!

Tamino and Pamina enter the temple.

ACT II - Scene 8

Daylight. A small garden. Papageno appears with a rope wrapped around his waist.

PAPAGENO::

Papagena! Papagena! Papagena!
Weibchen! Täubchen! Meine Schöne!
Vergebens! Ach, sie ist verloren!
Ich bin zum Unglück schon geboren!
Ich plauderte, und das war schlecht,
und drum geschieht es mir schon recht!

Seit ich gekostet diesen Wein,
seit ich das schöne Weibchen sah,
so brennt's im Herzenskämmerlein,
so zwickt's hier, so zwickt's da.

Papagena! Herzensweibchen!
Papagena, liebes Täubchen!
Es ist umsonst, es ist vergebens!
Müde bin ich meines Lebens!
Sterben macht der Lieb' ein End',
wenn's im Herzen noch so brennt.

Diesen Baum da will ich zieren,
mir an ihm den Hals zuschnüren,
weil das Leben mir mißfällt;
gute Nacht, du falsche Welt.
Weil du böse an mir handelst,
mir kein schönes Kind zubandelst,
so ist's aus, so sterbe ich;
schöne Mädchen, denkt an mich.

Will sich eine um mich Armen,
Eh' ich hänge, noch erbarmen,
Nun, so laß ich's diesmal sein!
Rufet nur, ja oder nein.

Keine hört mich; alles stille!
Also ist es euer Wille?
Papageno, frisch hinauf!
Ende deinen Lebenslauf!

Nun, ich warte noch, es sei,
Bis man zählet: eins, zwei, drei.

PAPAGENO:

Papagena! Papagena! Papagena!
Little woman! Little dove! My beauty!
It's hopeless! Ah, I've lost her!
I was born to be miserable!
I talked, and that was wrong,
so it serves me right!.

Since I tasted that wine and saw that
beautiful little woman, there has been a
constant fire burning in my heart
that's torturing me day and night!

Papagena! Light of my life!
Papagena, darling little dove!
It's no use, it's all hopeless!
I'm tired of life!
Nothing is left for me but to die,
even though my heart is burning.

(He takes the rope)
I've chosen this tree to hang from,
since life is no longer worth living.
Farewell deceitful world since you treated
me so badly, and refused to grant me a
beautiful mate, all is over and I shall die.
Lovely girl, remember me.

In case someone wants to love or pity me
before I hang myself,
just call out to me, yes or no.

(Papageno looks around)
No one hears me, all is quiet!
Tell me then, is it your will?
Papageno, swing up high!
End your life!
(He looks around)
Well, I'll wait a while.
I'll count from one, two, three.

Eins!

(He whistles)
One!

Zwei!

(He looks around and whistles)
Two!

Drei!

(He looks around and whistles)
Three!

Nun, wohlan, es bleibt dabei, weil mich
nichts zurücke hält, Gute Nacht, du falsche
Welt!

(He looks around)
Well then, let it be! While nothing is
stopping me, goodnight then you deceitful
world!

As Papageno tries to hang himself, the Three Youths hurry in.

DREI KNABEN:
Halt ein, o Papageno! und sei klug,
man lebt nur einmal, dies sei dir genug!

THE THREE YOUTHS:
Stop Papageno, be smart! You only live
once, and let that be enough for you!

PAPAGENO:
Ihr habt gut reden, habt gut scherzen;
doch brennt' es euch, wie mich im Herzen,
ihr würdet auch nach Mädchen gehn.

PAPAGENO:
It's easy for you to talk and joke. If your
hearts would burn like mine, you would
also chase young girls.

DREI KNABEN::
So lasse deine Glöckchen klingen,
dies wird dein Weibchen zu dir bringen.

THE THREE YOUTHS:
Then let your magic bells ring. They will
bring your little woman to you.

PAPAGENO::
Ich Narr vergaß der Zauberdinge!
Erklinge, Glockenspiel, erklinge!
Ich muß mein liebes Mädchen seh'n.
Klinget, Glöckchen, klinget,
Schafft mein Mädchen her!
Klinget, Glöckchen, klinget!
Bringt mein Weibchen her.

PAPAGENO:
I'm such a fool, I forgot the magic thing!
Ring, bells, ring!
I must see my dear little girl.
Ring little bells, ring!
Bring my little girl!
Ring, bells, ring!
Bring my little girl to me!

He plays the glockenspiel, and then the Three Youths return with Papagena.

DREI KNABEN:
Nun, Papageno, sieh dich um!

THREE YOUTHS:
Now, Papageno, turn around!

The Three Youths leave. Papageno turns around, sees Papagena,
and becomes dumbfounded.

PAPAGENO:
Pa-pa-pa-pa-pa-pa-Papagena!

PAPAGENO: *(dancing around her)*
Pa-Pa-Pa-Pa-Pa-Papagena!

PAPAGENA:
Pa-pa-pa-pa-pa-pa-Papageno!

PAPAGENA: *(dancing around him)*
Pa-Pa-Pa-Pa-Pa-Papageno!

BEIDE:
Pa-Pa-Pa-Pa-Pa-Papageno! Papagena!

BOTH:
Pa-Pa-Pa-Pa-Pa Papageno! Papagena!

PAPAGENO:
Bist du mir nun ganz gegeben?

PAPAGENO:
Are you really all mine now?

PAPAGENA:
Nun, bin ich dir ganz gegeben!

PAPAGENA:
Yes, I'm really all yours now!

PAPAGENO:
Nun, so sei mein liebes Weibchen!

PAPAGENO:
So then be my little wife!

PAPAGENA:
Nun, so sei mein Herzenstäubchen!

PAPAGENA:
Now then be my little sweetheart!

BEIDE:
Welche Freude wird das sein, wenn die
Götter uns bedenken, unsrer liebe Kinder
schenken, so liebe, kleine Kinderlein!

BOTH:
What a joy it would be if the gods would
bless us with children, very darling little
children!

PAPAGENO::
Erst einen kleinen Papageno.

PAPAGENO:
First a little Papageno.

PAPAGENA:
Dann eine kleine Papagena.

PAPAGENA:
Then a little Papagena.

PAPAGENO:
Dann wieder einen Papageno.

PAPAGENO:
Then another Papageno.

PAPAGENA:
Dann wieder eine Papagena-

PAPAGENA:
Then another Papagena.

BEIDE:
Papageno! Papagena!
Es ist das höchste der Gefühle,
wenn viele, viele Papageno/a,
der Eltern Segen werden sein.

BOTH:
Papagena! Papagena!
It would be the greatest feeling
if we would be blessed with many
Papagenos and Papagenas.

Both leave arm in arm.

ACT II - Scene 9

Rugged cliffs. It is dark. Monostatos, the Queen,
and the Three Ladies appear with lighted torches.

MONOSTATOS:
Nur stille, stille, stille,
bald dringen wir im Tempel ein.

MONOSTATOS: *(near the Queen)*
All is quiet, quiet, quiet!
Soon we will enter the temple.

ALLE::
Nur stille, stille, stille,
bald dringen wir im Tempel ein.

ALL THE LADIES:
All is quiet, quiet, quiet!
Soon we will enter the temple.

MONOSTATOS:
Doch, Fürstin, halte Wort!
Erfülle dein Kind muß meine Gattin sein.

MONOSTATOS:
You, Queen, will keep your word,
your child must become my wife!

KÖNIGIN:
Ich halte Wort; es ist mein Wille, mein Kind
soll deine Gattin sein.

QUEEN:
I keep my word, I want my child to be your
wife.

DREI DAMEN:
Ihr Kind soll deine Gattin sein.

ALL THE LADIES:
Her child will be his wife.

The sounds of thunder and rushing water are heard.

MONOSTATOS:
Doch still, ich höre schrecklich Rauschen,
wie Donnerton und Wasserfall.

MONOSTATOS:
Quiet! I hear a frightful roaring, like
thunder and a waterfall.

KÖNIGIN, DIE DAMEN:
Ja, fürchterlich ist dieses Rauschen,
Wie fernen Donners Widerhall!

QUEEN AND LADIES:
Yes, this roaring is horrible, like the echo of
distant thunder!

MONOSTATOS:
Nun sind sie in des Tempels Hallen.

MONOSTATOS:
Now they're assembling in the temple hall.

ALLE::
Dort wollen wir sie überfallen. Die
Frömmler tilgen von der Erd' mit
Feuersglut und mächt'gem Schwert.

ALL:
We will overtake them there. We will
destroy them with sword and fire, and
remove those hypocrites from the earth.

DREI DAMEN, MONOSTATOS:
Dir, große Königin der Nacht,
sei uns'rer Rache Opfer gebracht.

LADIES AND MONOSTATOS:
To satisfy your vengeance, we will bring the
victims to you, great Queen of the Night.

Thunder, lightning, and storm.

ALLE::
Zerschmettert, zernichtet ist unsere Macht,
Wir alle gestürzt in ewige Nacht!

ALL:
Our power is destroyed and demolished,
and we'll be hurled into eternal darkness!

They all sink into the earth.

ACT II - Scene 10

Temple of the Sun. Sarastro, Priests and Priestesses.
Tamino and Pamina stand before Sarastro.

SARASTRO:
Die Strahlen der Sonne vertreiben die
Nacht, Zernichten der Heuchler
erschlichene Macht.

SARASTRO:
The sun's radiant glory has vanquished the
night, and has destroyed the deceiving
powers of the hypocrites.

CHOR::
Heil sei euch Geweihten!
Ihr dränget durch Nacht.
Dank sei dir, Osiris,
Dank dir, Isis, gebracht!
Es siegte die Stärke
Und krönet zum Lohn
Die Schönheit und Weisheit
Mit ewiger Kron'.

CHORUS OF PRIESTS:
Glory to the consecrated!
You have been guided through darkness,
thanks to Osiris,
and thanks to Isis.
The strong have conquered,
and as their reward,
they are crowned
with eternal beauty and wisdom.

Ende

THE END

THE MAGIC FLUTE

Discography

1937   (Live performance from the Salzburg Festival)
          Novotna (Pamina); Roswaenge (Tamino);
          Domgraf-Fassbaender (Papageno); Komarek (Papagena);
          Osvath (Queen); Kipnis (Saarastro); Jerger (Elderly Priest);
          Vienna State Opera Orchestra and Chorus;
          Toscanini (Conductor)

1937   Lemnitz (Pamina); Roswaenge (Tamino); Hüsch (Papageno);
          Beilke (Papagena); Berger (Queen); Strienz (Sarastro);
          Grossmann (Elderly Priest); Tessmer (Monostatos);
          Berlin Philharmonic/Berlin Favres Chorus;
          Beecham (Conductor)

1950   Seefried (Pamina); Dermota (Tamino); Kunz (Papageno);
          Loose Papagena); Lipp (Queen); Weber (Sarastro);
          London (Elderly Priest); Klein (Monostatos);
          Vienna State Opera Orchestra and Chorus;
          Karajan (Conductor)

1951   (Live performance from Salzburg Festival)
          Seefried (Pamina); Dermota (Tamino); Kunz (Papageno);
          Oravez (Papagena); Lipp (Queen); Greindl (Sarastro);
          Schöffler (Elderly Priest); Klein (Monostatos);
          Vienna State Opera Orchestra and Chorus;
          Furtwängler (Conductor)

1955   Stader (Pamina); Haefliger (Tamino); Fischer-Dieskay (Papageno);
          Otto (Papagena); Streich (Queen); Greindl (Sarastro);
          Borg (Elderly Priest); Vantin (Monostatos);
          Berlin Radio Symphony Orchestra/Berlin RIAS Chorus;
          Fricasy (Conductor)

1955   Gueden (Pamina); Simoneau (Tamino); Berry (Papageno);
          Loos (Papagena); Böhme (Sarastro); Schöffler (Elderly Priest);
          Jaresch (Monostatos);
          Vienna State Opera Chorus and Orchestra;
          Böhn (Conductor)

1955   Bijster (Pamina); Garen (Tamino); Gschwend (Papageno);
          Duval (Papagena); Tyler (Queen) Hoekman (Sarastro);
          Goren (Elderly Priest); Taverne (Monostatos);
          Netherlands Philharmonic Orchestra
          Krannhals (Conductor)

1964   Janowitz (Pamina); Gedda (Tamino); Berry (Papageno);
        Pütz (Papagena); Popp (Queen); Frick (Sarastro);
        Crass (Elderly Priest); Unger (Monostatos);
        Philharmonia Chorus and Orchestra;
        Klemperer (Conductor)

1965   Lear (Pamina); Wunderlich (Tamino); Fischer-Dieskau (Papageno);
        Otto (Papagena); Peters (Queen); Crass (Sarastro);
        Hotter (Elderly Priest); Lenz (Monostatos);
        Berlin Philharmonic/Berlin RIAS Chorus;
        Böhn (COnductor)

1968   Donath (Pamina); Schreier (Tamino); Leib (Papageno);
        Geszty (Papagena); Adam (Sarastro); Vogel (Elderly Priest);
        Neukirch (Monostatos);
        Dresden State Orchestra/Leipzig Radio Chorus;
        Suitner (Conductor)

1969   Lorengar (Pamina); Burrows (Tamino); Prey (Papageno);
        Holm (Papagena); Deutekom (Queen); Talvela (Sarastro);
        Fischer-Dieskau (Elderly Priest); Stolze (Monostatos);
        Vienna State Opera Chorus and Orchestra;
        Solti (Conductor)

1972   Rothenberger (Pamina); Schreier (Tamino); Berry (Papageno);
        Miljakovic (Papagena); Moser (Queen); Moll (Sarastro);
        Adam (Elderly Priest); Brokmeier (Monostatos);
        Bavarian State Opera Chorus and Orchestra;
        Sawallisch (Conductor)

1974   (Sound track in Swedish)
        Urrila (Pamina); Köstlinger (Tamino); Hagegärd (Papageno);
        Eriksson (Papagena); Nordin (Queen); Cold (Sarastro);
        Saedén (Elderly Priest); Ulfung (Monostatos);
        Swedish Radio Orchestra and Chorus;
        Ericson (Conductor)

1978   Te Kanawa (Pamina); Hofmann (Tamino); Huttenlocher (Papageno);
        Battle (Papagena); Gruberova (Queen); Moll (Sarastro);
        Van Dam (Elderly Priest); Orth (Monostatos);
        Rhine Opera Chorus/Strasbourg Philharmonic Orchestra;
        Lombard (Conductor)

1980   Mathis (Pamina); Araiza (Tamino); Hornik (Papageno);
        Perry (Papagena); Van Dam (Sarastro); Kruse (Monostatos);
        Berlin Philharmonic/Deutsche Oper Chorus;
        Karajan (Conductor)

1980   Cortrubas (Pamina); Tappy (Tamino); Boesch (Papageno);
        Kales (Papagena); Talvela (Sarastro); Hiestermann (Monostatos);
        Vienna State Opera Chorus and Orchestra;
        Levine (Conductor)

1981   Popp (Pamina); Jerusalem (Tamino); Brendel (Papageno);
        Lindner (Papagena); Gruberova (Queen); Bracht (Sarastro);
        Zednik (Monosstatos);
        Bavarian Radio Chorus and Sympony Orchestra;
        Haitink (Conductor)

1982   Kwebsilber (Pamina); de Mey (Tamino); Verschaeve (Papageno);
        Putten (Papagena); Poulenard (Queen); der Kamp (Sarastro);
        Vels (Monostatos);
        Viva la Musica Chamber Choir/Utrech/Amsterdam Baroque Orchestra;
        Koopman (Conductor)

1984   M. Price (Pamina) Schreier (Tamino); Melbye (Papageno);
        Venuti (Papagena); Serra (Queen); Moll (Sarastro);
        Tear (Monostatos);
        Leipzig Radio Chorus/Dresden State Orchestra;
        Davis (Conductor)

1988   Bonney (Pamina); Blochwitz (Tamino); Scharinger (Papageno);
        Schmid (Papagena); Gruberova (Queen); Salminen (Saarastro);
        Keller (Monostatos);
        Zurich Opera Hourse Chorus and Orchestra;
        Harnoncourt (Conductor)

1989   Orgonasova (Pamina); Winbergh (Tamino); Hagegärd (Papageno);
        Bovet (Papagena); Sumi Jo (Queen); Selig (Sarastro);
        Vogel (Monostatos);
        Paris Orchestra Ensemble/ROmand Chamber Choir;
        Jordan (Conductor)

1989   Te Kanawa (Pamina(; Araiza (Tamino); Bär (Papageno);
          Lind (Papagena); Studer (Queen); Ramey (Sarastro);
          Baldin (Monostatos);
          Abrosian Opera Chorus/Academy of St. Martin in the Fields Orchestra;
          Mariner (Conductor)

1990   Ziesak (Pamina); Heilmann (Tamino); Krauss (Papageno);
          Leitner (Papagena); Sumi Jo (Queen); Moll (Sarastro);
          Zednik (Monostatos);
          Vienna State Opera Orchestra and Chorus;
          Solti (Conductor)

1990   Upshaw (Pamina); Johnson (Tamino); Schmidt (Papageno);
          Pierard (Papagena); Hoch (Queen); Hauptmann (Sarastro);
          de Mey (Monostatos);
          London Classical Players/Schütz Choir of London;
          Norrington (Conductor)

1991   Hendricks (Pamina); Hadley (Tamino); Allen (Papageno);
          Steinsky (Papagena); Anderson (Queen); Lloyd (Sarastro);
          Wildhaber (Monostatos);
          Scottish Chamber Orchestra and Chorus;
          Mackerras (Conductor)

THE MAGIC FLUTE

Videography

Phillips VHS:

>Popp (Pamina); Araiza (Tamino); Brendel (Papageno);
>Gruberova (Queen); Moll (Sarastro); Rootering (Elderly Priest); Orth
>(Monostatos);
>Bavarian State Opera Orchestra and Chorus;
>Sawallisch (Conductor);
>Everding (Director);
>Windgassen (Video Director)

DG VHS:

>Battle (Pamina); Araiza (Tamino); Hemm (Papageno); Serra (Queen);
>Moll (Sarastro); Schmidt (Elderly Priest);
>Metropolitan Opera Chorus and Orchestra;
>Levine (Conductor);
>Cox and Mostart (Directors);
>Large (Video Director);

Virgin VHS:

>Biel (Pamina); Dahlberg (Tamino); Samuelsson (Papageno);
>Frandsen (Queen); Polgár (Sarastro); Salomaa (Elderly Priest);
>Chorus and Orchestra of the Drottninghom Court Theatre;
>Ostman (Conductor);
>Järvefelt (Director);
>Oloffson (Video Director)

Phillips VHS:

>M. Price (Pamina); Scheier (Tamino); Melbye (Papageno);
>Serra (Queen); Moll (Sarastro); Adam (Elderly Priest);
>Tear (Monostatos);
>Leipzig Radio Chorus/Dresden Staatskapelle;
>Davis (Conductor);
>Groot (Animator)

DICTIONARY OF OPERA AND MUSICAL TERMS

Accelerando - Play the music faster, but gradually.

Adagio - At slow or gliding tempo, not as slow as Largo, but not as fast as Andante.

Agitato - Restless or agitated.

Allegro - At a brisk or lively tempo, faster than Andante but not as fast as Presto.

Andante - A moderately slow, easy-going tempo.

Appoggiatura - An extra or embellishing note preceding a main melodic note or tone. Usually written as a note of smaller size, it shares the time value of the main note.

Arabesque - Flourishes or fancy patterns usually applying to vocal virtuosity.

Aria - A solo song usually structured in a formal pattern. Arias generally convey reflective and introspective thoughts rather than descriptive action.

Arietta - A shortened form of aria.

Arioso - A musical passage or composition having a mixture of free recitative and metrical song.

Arpeggio - Producing the tones of a chord in succession but not simultaneously.

Atonal - Music that is not anchored in traditional musical tonality; it uses the chromatic scale impartially, does not use the diatonic scale and has no keynote or tonal center.

Ballad Opera - 18th century English opera consisting of spoken dialogue and music derived from popular ballad and folksong sources. The most famous is *The Beggar's Opera* which was a satire of the Italian opera seria.

Bar - A vertical line across the stave that divides the music into units.

Baritone - A male singing voice ranging between the bass and tenor.

Baroque - A style of artistic expression prevalent in the 17th century that is marked generally by the use of complex forms, bold ornamentation, and florid decoration. The Baroque period extends from approximately 1600 to 1750 and includes the works of the original creators of modern opera, the Camerata, as well as the later works by Bach and Handel.

Bass - The lowest male voices, usually divided into categories such as:

> **Basso buffo -** A bass voice that specializes in comic roles like Dr. Bartolo in Rossini's *The Barber of Seville.*

> **Basso cantante** - A bass voice that demonstrates melodic singing quality rather than comic or tragic: King Philip in Verdi's *Don Carlos.*

> **Basso profundo -** the deepest, most profound, or most dramatic of bass voices: Sarastro in Mozart's *The Magic Flute.*

Bel canto - Literally "beautiful singing." It originated in Italian opera of the 17th and 18th centuries and stressed beautiful tones produced with ease, clarity, purity, evenness, together with an agile vocal technique and virtuosity. Bel canto flourished in the first half of the 19th century in the works of Rossini, Bellini, and Donizetti.

Cabaletta - Typically a lively bravura extension of an aria or duet that creates a climax. The term is derived from the Italian word "cavallo," or horse: it metaphorically describes a horse galloping to the finish line.

Cadenza - A flourish or brilliant part of an aria commonly inserted just before a finale.

Camerata - A gathering of Florentine writers and musicians between 1590 and 1600 who attempted to recreate what they believed was the ancient Greek theatrical synthesis of drama, music, and stage spectacle; their experimentation led to the creation of the early structural forms of modern opera.

Cantabile - An expression indication urging the singer to sing sweetly.

Cantata - A choral piece generally containing Scriptural narrative texts: Bach Cantatas.

Cantilena - A lyrical melodic line meant to be played or sung "cantabile," or with sweetness and expression.

Canzone - A short, lyrical operatic song usually containing no narrative association with the drama but rather simply reflecting the character's state of mind: Cherubino's "Voi che sapete" in Mozart's *The Marriage of Figaro.* Shorter versions are called canzonettas.

Castrato - A young male singer who was surgically castrated to retain his treble voice.

Cavatina - A short aria popular in the 18th century without the da capo repeat section.

Classical Period - The period between the Baroque and Romantic periods. The Classical period is generally considered to have begun with the birth of Mozart (1756) and ended with Beethoven's death (1830). Stylistically, the music of the period stressed clarity, precision, and rigid structural forms.

Coda - A trailer or tailpiece added on by the composer after the music's natural conclusion.

Coloratura - Literally colored: it refers to a soprano singing in the bel canto tradition with great agility, virtuosity, embellishments and ornamentation: Joan Sutherland singing in Donizetti's *Lucia di Lammermoor.*

Commedia dell'arte - A popular form of dramatic presentation originating in Renaissance Italy in which highly stylized characters were involved in comic plots involving mistaken identities and misunderstandings. The standard characters were Harlequin and Colombine: The "play within a play" in Leoncavallo's *I Pagliacci.*

Comprimario - A singer portraying secondary character roles such as confidantes, servants, and messengers.

Continuo - A bass part (as for a keyboard or stringed instrument) that was used especially in baroque ensemble music; it consists of a succession of bass notes with figures that indicate the required chords. Also called *figured bass, thoroughbass.*

Contralto - The lowest female voice derived from "contra" against, and "alto" voice, a voice between the tenor and mezzo-soprano.

Countertenor, or male alto vocal range - A high male voice generally singing within the female high soprano ranges.

Counterpoint - The combination of one or more independent melodies added into a single harmonic texture in which each retains its linear character: polyphony. The most sophisticated form of counterpoint is the fugue form in which up to 6 to 8 voices are combined, each providing a variation on the basic theme but each retaining its relation to the whole.

Crescendo - A gradual increase in the volume of a musical passage.

Da capo - Literally "from the top": repeat. Early 17th century da capo arias were in the form of A B A, the last A section repeating the first A section.

Deus ex machina - Literally "god out of a machine." A dramatic technique in which a person or thing appears or is introduced suddenly and unexpectedly; it provides a contrived solution to an apparently insoluble dramatic difficulty.

Diatonic - Relating to a major or minor musical scale that comprises intervals of five whole steps and two half steps.

Diminuendo - Gradually getting softer, the opposite of crescendo.

Dissonance - A mingling of discordant sounds that do not harmonize within the diatonic scale.

Diva - Literally a "goddess"; generally refers to a female opera star who either possesses, or pretends to possess, great rank.

Dominant - The fifth tone of the diatonic scale: in the key of C, the dominant is G.

Dramma giocoso - Literally meaning amusing, or lighthearted. Like tragicomedy it represents an opera whose story combines both serious and comic elements: Mozart's *Don Giovanni*.

Falsetto - Literally a lighter or "false" voice; an artificially produced high singing voice that extends above the range of the full voice.

Fioritura - Literally "flower"; a flowering ornamentation or embellishment of the vocal line within an aria.

Forte, Fortissimo - Forte (*f*) means loud: mezzo forte (*mf*) is fairly loud; fortissimo (*ff*) even louder, and additional *fff*'s indicate greater degrees of loudness.

Glissando - A rapid sliding up or down the scale.

Grand Opera - An opera in which there is no spoken dialogue and the entire text is set to music, frequently treating serious and dramatic subjects. Grand Opera flourished in France in the 19th century (Meyerbeer) and most notably by Verdi (Aida): the genre is epic in scale and combines spectacle, large choruses, scenery, and huge orchestras.

Heldentenor - A tenor with a powerful dramatic voice who possesses brilliant top notes and vocal stamina. Heldentenors are well suited to heroic (Wagnerian) roles: Lauritz Melchoir in Wagner's *Tristan und Isolde*.

Imbroglio - Literally "Intrigue"; an operatic scene with chaos and confusion and appropriate diverse melodies and rhythms.

Largo or larghetto - Largo indicates a very slow tempo; Larghetto is slightly faster than Largo.

Legato - Literally "tied"; therefore, successive tones that are connected smoothly. Opposing Legato would be Marcato (strongly accented and punctuated) and Staccato (short and aggressive).

Leitmotif - A short musical passage attached to a person, thing, feeling, or idea that provides associations when it recurs or is recalled.

Libretto - Literally "little book"; the text of an opera. On Broadway, the text of songs is called "lyrics" but the spoken text in the play is called the "book."

Lied - A German song; the plural is "lieder." Originally German art songs of the 19th century.

Light opera, or operetta - Operas that contain comic elements but light romantic plots: Johann Strauss's _Die Fledermaus_.

Maestro - From the Italian "master": a term of respect to conductors, composers, directors, and great musicians.

Melodrama - Words spoken over music. Melodrama appears in Beethoven's _Fidelio_ but flourished during the late 19th century in the operas of Massenet (_Manon_). Melodrama should not be confused with melodrama when it describes a work that is characterized by extravagant theatricality and by the predominance of plot and physical action over characterization.

Mezza voce - Literally "medium voice," or singing with medium or half volume; it is generally intended as a vocal means to intensify emotion.

Mezzo-soprano - A woman's voice with a range between that of the soprano and contralto.

Molto - Very. Molto agitato means very agitated.

Obbligato - An elaborate accompaniment to a solo or principal melody that is usually played by a single instrument.

Octave - A musical interval embracing eight diatonic degrees: therefore, from C to C is an octave.

Opera - Literally "a work"; a dramatic or comic play combining music.

Opera buffa - Italian comic opera that flourished during the bel canto era. Buffo characters were usually basses singing patter songs: Dr. Bartolo in Rossini's _The Barber of Seville,_ and Dr. Dulcamara in Donizetti's _The Elixir of Love._

Opéra comique - A French opera characterized by spoken dialogue interspersed between the arias and ensemble numbers, as opposed to Grand Opera in which there is no spoken dialogue.

Operetta, or light opera - Operas that contain comic elements but tend to be more romantic: Strauss's *Die Fledermaus,* Offenbach's *La Périchole*, and Lehar's *The Merry Widow*. In operettas, there is usually much spoken dialogue, dancing, practical jokes, and mistaken identities.

Oratorio - A lengthy choral work, usually of a religious or philosophical nature and consisting chiefly of recitatives, arias, and choruses but in deference to its content, performed without action or scenery: Handel's *Messiah*.

Ornamentation - Extra embellishing notes—appoggiaturas, trills, roulades, or cadenzas—that enhance a melodic line.

Overture - The orchestral introduction to a musical dramatic work that frequently incorporates musical themes within the work.

Parlando - Literally "speaking"; the imitation of speech while singing, or singing that is almost speaking over the music. It is usually short and with minimal orchestral accompaniment.

Patter - Words rapidly and quickly delivered. Figaro's Largo in Rossini's *The Barber of Seville* is a patter song.

Pentatonic - A five-note scale, like the black notes within an octave on the piano.

Piano - Soft volume.

Pitch - The property of a musical tone that is determined by the frequency of the waves producing it.

Pizzicato - A passage played by plucking the strings instead of stroking the string with the bow.

Polyphony - Literally "many voices." A style of musical composition in which two or more independent melodies are juxtaposed in harmony; counterpoint.

Polytonal - The use of several tonal schemes simultaneously.

Portamento - A continuous gliding movement from one tone to another.

Prelude - An orchestral introduction to an act or the whole opera. An Overture can appear only at the beginning of an opera.

Presto, Prestissimo - Very fast and vigorous.

Prima Donna - The female star of an opera cast. Although the term was initially used to differentiate between the dramatic and vocal importance of a singer, today it generally describes the personality of a singer rather than her importance in the particular opera.

Prologue - A piece sung before the curtain goes up on the opera proper: Tonio's Prologue in Leoncavallo's *I Pagliacci*.

Quaver - An eighth note.

Range - The divisions of the voice: soprano, mezzo-soprano, contralto, tenor, baritone, and bass.

Recitative - A formal device that that advances the plot. It is usually a rhythmically free vocal style that imitates the natural inflections of speech; it represents the dialogue and narrative in operas and oratorios. Secco recitative is accompanied by harpsichord and sometimes with cello or continuo instruments and *accompagnato* indicates that the recitative is accompanied by the orchestra.

Ritornello - A short recurrent instrumental passage between elements of a vocal composition.

Romanza - A solo song that is usually sentimental; it is usually shorter and less complex than an aria and rarely deals with terror, rage, and anger.

Romantic Period - The period generally beginning with the raiding of the Bastille (1789) and the last revolutions and uprisings in Europe (1848). Romanticists generally found inspiration in nature and man. Beethoven's *Fidelio* (1805) is considered the first Romantic opera, followed by the works of Verdi and Wagner.

Roulade - A florid vocal embellishment sung to one syllable.

Rubato - Literally "robbed"; it is a fluctuation of tempo within a musical phrase, often against a rhythmically steady accompaniment.

Secco - The accompaniment for recitative played by the harpsichord and sometimes continuo instruments.

Semitone - A half-step, the smallest distance between two notes. In the key of C, the notes are E and F, and B and C.

Serial music - Music based on a series of tones in a chosen pattern without regard for traditional tonality.

Sforzando - Sudden loudness and force; it must stick out from the texture and provide a shock.

Singspiel - Early German musical drama employing spoken dialogue between songs: Mozart's *The Magic Flute*.

Soprano - The highest range of the female voice ranging from lyric (light and graceful quality) to dramatic (fuller and heavier in tone).

Sotto voce - Literally "below the voice"; sung softly between a whisper and a quiet conversational tone.

Soubrette - A soprano who sings supporting roles in comic opera: Adele in Strauss's *Die Fledermaus*, or Despina in Mozart's *Così fan tutte*.

Spinto - From the Italian "spingere" (to push); a soprano having lyric vocal qualities who "pushes" the voice to achieve heavier dramatic qualities.

Sprechstimme - Literally "speak voice." The singer half sings a note and half speaks; the declamation sounds like speaking but the duration of pitch makes it seem almost like singing.

Staccato - Short, clipped, rapid articulation; the opposite of the caressing effects of legato.

Stretto - A concluding passage performed in a quicker tempo to create a musical climax.

Strophe - Music repeated for each verse of an aria.

Syncopation - Shifting the beat forward or back from its usual place in the bar; it is a temporary displacement of the regular metrical accent in music caused typically by stressing the weak beat.

Supernumerary - A "super"; a performer with a non-singing role: "Spear-carrier."

Tempo - Time, or speed. The ranges are Largo for very slow to Presto for very fast.

Tenor - Highest natural male voice.

Tessitura - The general range of a melody or voice part; but specifically, the part of the register in which most of the tones of a melody or voice part lie.

Tonality - The organization of all the tones and harmonies of a piece of music in relation to a tonic (the first tone of its scale).

Tone Poem - An orchestral piece with a program; a script.

Tonic - The keynote of the key in which a piece is written. C is the tonic of C major.

Trill - Two adjacent notes rapidly and repeatedly alternated.

Tutti - All together.

Twelve tone - The 12 chromatic tones of the octave placed in a chosen fixed order and constituting with some permitted permutations and derivations the melodic and harmonic material of a serial musical piece. Each note of the chromatic scale is used as part of the melody before any other note gets repeated.

Verismo - Literally "truth"; the artistic use of contemporary everyday material in preference to the heroic or legendary in opera. A movement from the late 19th century: *Carmen.*

Vibrato - A "vibration"; a slightly tremulous effect imparted to vocal or instrumental tone for added warmth and expressiveness by slight and rapid variations in pitch.